REPAIR & RENOVATE

Rugby Site

kitchens

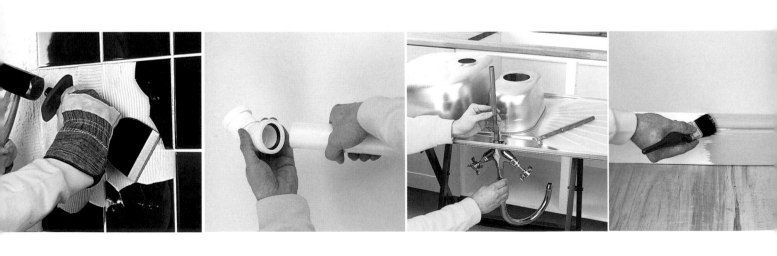

REPAIR & RENOVATE

kitchens

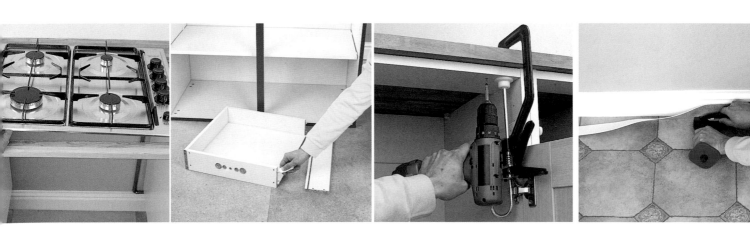

Julian Cassell & Peter Parham

MURDOCH
B O O K S

kitchens **contents**

Changing the look of a splashback could not be easier –
simply paint over or attach new tiles directly, see page 135.

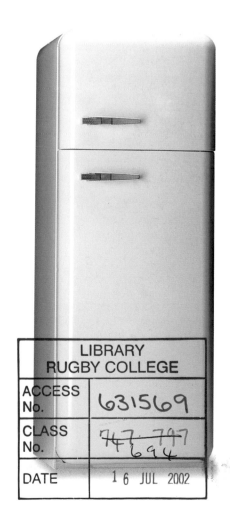

introduction

Home improvement is fast becoming a national pastime, with more and more enthusiasts choosing to undertake jobs that used to be left to professional tradespeople. Taking on a project yourself and seeing it through from planning to final decoration can be more rewarding than hiring someone else and ensures that the finished effect is how you envisaged – and with minimal labour costs there are real savings to be made.

considering renovations

When browsing through lifestyle magazines or viewing the sets on show in home improvement outlets it is easy to appreciate the great improvements and innovations in kitchen design of recent years. What was once the domain of the housewife has now become a communal living area, providing a practical space for food preparation while also delivering good looks and style.

By far the largest section of the market is occupied by fitted kitchens, which, by integrating storage facilities and appliances into one or more runs of units with a common style and finish, make the best possible use of space and provide a pleasing uniformity of style. The fitted look has advanced to such an extent that many appliances, such as dishwashers, can be housed in special units to blend seamlessly with the rest of the kitchen. Developments in

appliance technology mean it is also rare to find a kitchen that has only a cooker and sink – a number of different cooking appliances are now common and often the sink merely functions as a source of water with dishwashers having taken over the function of washing up.

With the DIY home improvement revolution, many people are now also beginning to tackle jobs that were once the domain of professional tradespeople, and the area of kitchen installation is by no means an exception to this rule. Indeed, manufacturers have done their utmost to build units and fittings that can be installed by any competent home improvement enthusiast. Most complete kitchen furniture kits follow the design principle whereby fitting is a logical process of systematically building up the new kitchen, unit by unit, in the correct order. Much of this book is therefore involved with describing the correct procedures for planning, preparing, fitting and finishing a new kitchen in order to achieve the best results.

planning, fitting & finishing

Before setting out on a complete kitchen renovation project, it is important to have a sound appreciation of the way in which you interact with the kitchen in your daily life. Once you understand how it functions at present, you will then be able to gauge the extent to which the design of the kitchen can be changed to improve the efficiency of its functioning. It may be that the existing layout of units and appliances is adequate and a simple update in style is all that is required. Or you may decide the layout needs something of a rethink, in which case it is important to have a full understanding of kitchen anatomy and how layout may be planned to accommodate different needs. Providing a complete overview of kitchen design,

LEFT *The installation of a hood-and-chimney fan has turned the cooker into the visual focal point of this run of units.*

chapter 1 considers the factors that may influence the choice of layout – such as the way in which electrical, water and gas supplies will need to be routed to the relevant appliances – and demonstrates how the best use can be made of the available space in different shaped kitchens. This chapter also investigates the options available for unfitted kitchens and the possibilities for combining both fitted and unfitted looks to create the ideal finish.

Carrying out improvement work in the kitchen will almost certainly disrupt the day-to-day activities of a household. It is therefore important to plan very carefully any renovation so that disruption may be kept to a minimum. Chapter 2 considers the issues you will need to take into account for successful planning and also looks at the options available for types of unit, appliances, accessories and worktop material to help you make your final choice. Even if you are going to carry out the majority of the work yourself, it is

still likely that you will need to seek help from professional tradespeople at some stage. For example, you may feel that dealing with electrical and plumbing supplies is a job better left to the professionals – it is certainly the case that adjustments to gas pipes should only be attempted by a qualified fitter. Chapter 2 therefore also considers how best to liaise with professional tradespeople to ensure the work is carried out speedily, effectively and at a reasonable price.

Having thoroughly planned and coordinated the renovation, getting down to work is simply a matter of methodically following the right techniques and correct procedures for fitting a kitchen. Chapters 3 and 4 demonstrate the procedures for installing almost every type of unit,

BELOW *Although this kitchen is predominantly fitted, the inclusion of an island unit introduces an unfitted element that complements the rustic feel to the kitchen.*

accessory and appliance you may encounter. There are always slight variations in manufacture, but you will find that most kitchen furniture designs share a great deal of construction principles and fitting procedures. Thus the techniques described in this book will cover most designs with only minor refinements in some instances, providing you with a comprehensive, step-by-step guide to kitchen renovation and also covering areas that the manufacturers' instruction manuals may leave out.

Once the actual units are fitted, attention must be turned to other surfaces in the room. If you are fitting an entirely new kitchen, it is likely that floor and wall finishes will also require updating or replacing. Surfaces in a kitchen environment must withstand considerable wear and tear, and you will need to balance decoration with durability when making your choice of finishing materials. Chapters 5 and 6 consider these areas and provide all the necessary guidance on choosing and fitting the ideal flooring and other decorative finishes for your kitchen.

repair & restoration

The last two chapters in the book show you how to carry out the most common minor repairs and detail several ways in which an existing kitchen may be revamped without going to the lengths of a total refit. Thus demonstrating how, with a limited investment on even the smallest of budgets, most kitchens may be returned to good working order or updated to provide a whole new look.

Whatever your aspirations may be, however large or small the kitchen renovation project you intend, or whether you are an inexperienced novice or a seasoned pro, this book will help at every stage – comprehensively guiding you through the renovation process to help you achieve the attractive and efficient kitchen you desire.

BELOW *The look of a kitchen is often determined by the style and colour of the door and drawer fronts.*

The layout of this book has been designed to provide project instruction in as comprehensive yet straightforward a manner as possible. The illustration featured below provides a guideline to the different elements incorporated into the page design. Full colour photos and diagrams combined with explanatory text, laid out in a clear, step-by-step order, provide easy-to-follow instructions. Each project is prefaced by a blue box containing a list of tools so that you will know in advance the range of equipment required for the job. Other boxes of additional text accompany each project, which are aimed at drawing your attention to particular issues. Pink safety boxes alert the reader to issues of safety and detail any precautions that may need to be taken. They also indicate where a particular job must be carried out by a tradesperson. Green tip boxes offer professional hints for the best way to go about a particular task involved in the project. Boxes with an orange border describe alternative options and techniques, which are relevant to the project in hand but not demonstrated on the page.

difficulty rating

The following symbols are designed to give an indication of difficulty level relating to particular tasks and projects in this book. Clearly what are simple jobs to one person may be difficult to another, and vice versa. These guidelines are primarily based on the ability of an individual in relation to the experience and degree of technical ability required.

Straightforward and requires limited technical skills

Straightforward but requires a reasonable skill level

Technically quite difficult, and could involve a number of skills

High skill level required and involves a number of techniques

safety boxes, coloured pink for emphasis, draw attention to the safety considerations for each project

options boxes offer additional instruction on techniques related to the project in hand

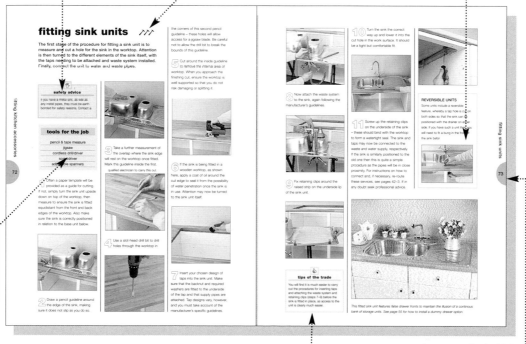

a list of tools has been provided at the beginning of each project

tip boxes have been used to provide helpful hints, developed from experience, on the best way to achieve particular tasks

colour-coordinated tabs help you quickly find your place again when moving between chapters

anatomy of kitchens

A kitchen is a working room in the home where specific tasks are performed, and as a result many of the design features, such as cooking facilities, sink units and worktops, are common to all types of kitchen. It is important to understand how these features interact so that they can be positioned to ensure that best use is made of available space. This chapter considers the vital components that make up the majority of kitchens and how design is tailored to meet requirements. In addition, this chapter will look at the 'invisible' parts of a kitchen, that is, the various household supplies that will need to be routed to appliances so that the kitchen facilities can function effectively.

The anatomy of this kitchen includes a complex layout, water and gas supplies, and both fitted and unfitted units.

the basic shape of a kitchen

Obviously, the size and dimensions of a room set constraints on the shape of a kitchen, but how space is utilized will also determine both its look and efficient operation. Kitchen design is based around three main areas: food storage and preparation, cooking, and washing. All three need to be positioned to enable the efficient and safe preparation of meals. The 'working triangle' of kitchen design reveals how these three areas best interact, showing the ideal positions for fridge and preparation areas in relation to the cooker and the sink. The illustrations on these pages demonstrate how this working triangle applies to three common kitchen shapes.

U-shaped kitchens

This type of kitchen shape provides probably the most satisfactory example of all for a working triangle. Distances between all three points are kept almost equal, which allows for optimum movement and access. The U-shaped design is most commonly found in large kitchens, although the same principles may also be applied to smaller kitchens where floor space is much more limited, and a similar working triangle shape can still be maintained.

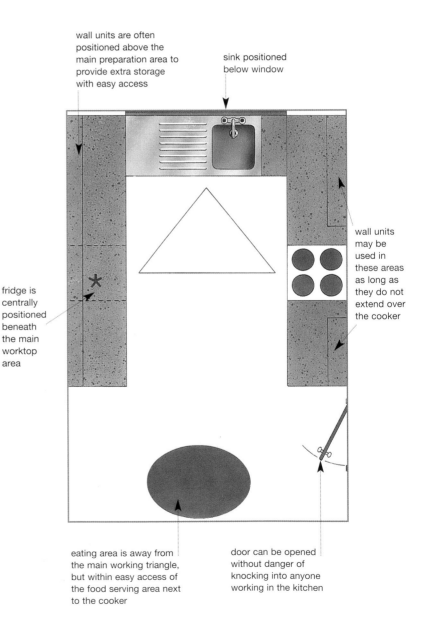

wall units are often positioned above the main preparation area to provide extra storage with easy access

sink positioned below window

wall units may be used in these areas as long as they do not extend over the cooker

fridge is centrally positioned beneath the main worktop area

eating area is away from the main working triangle, but within easy access of the food serving area next to the cooker

door can be opened without danger of knocking into anyone working in the kitchen

GALLEY KITCHENS

A galley-style kitchen is another popular design, similar to the U-shaped kitchen but more suitable for a narrow room. Galleys have units on the opposing longer walls but not on the opposing shorter walls. The working triangle in this situation does still bear similarities to that of the U-shaped kitchen, indeed some U-shaped kitchens are often referred to as galley kitchens, especially when the 'U' is particularly elongated and floor space between the two opposing longer runs of units is limited. In a traditional galley kitchen, however, the sink would be moved onto one of the longer walls, while still ensuring that a good working triangle, with fairly even dimensions, is maintained.

L-shaped kitchens

As the name suggests, the units in an L-shaped kitchen cover the majority of two adjacent walls in the room. The working triangle can still be maintained, although distances between the three points are no longer equal. Depending upon room size, it should still be possible to include an eating area in the kitchen.

tips of the trade

Sink position – In most kitchens the sink tends to be positioned underneath a window. The main reason for this is to provide a view when menial tasks are being carried out at the sink. However, positioning a sink below a window also guarantees that it is on an outside wall, and this makes it much easier to link the waste pipes to an outside drain.

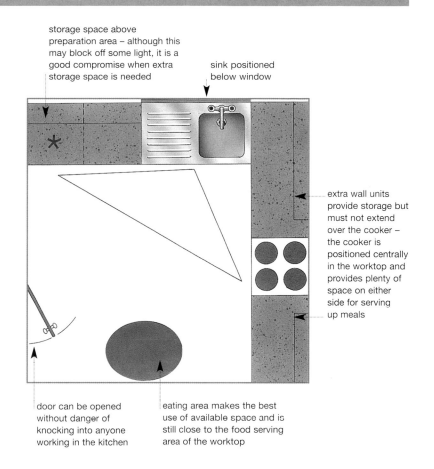

storage space above preparation area – although this may block off some light, it is a good compromise when extra storage space is needed

sink positioned below window

extra wall units provide storage but must not extend over the cooker – the cooker is positioned centrally in the worktop and provides plenty of space on either side for serving up meals

door can be opened without danger of knocking into anyone working in the kitchen

eating area makes the best use of available space and is still close to the food serving area of the worktop

13

single run kitchens

These are simple in design and are often used in long, narrow kitchens where the inclusion of double-facing units is impossible due to space limitations. In some cases, however, this choice of kitchen shape is used when budgetary concerns are paramount, and a simple limited stretch of units is all that is required. Despite the fact that the units and accessories are positioned along one wall, it can still be possible to maintain a working triangle, although the dimensions of the triangle will have to be considerably elongated to fit in with the kitchen design.

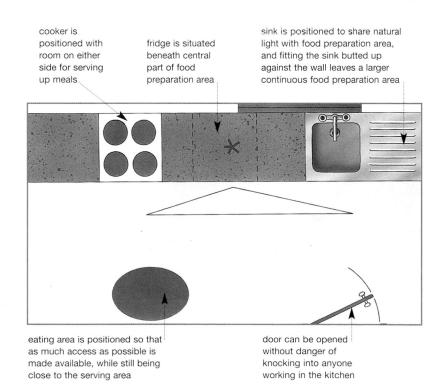

cooker is positioned with room on either side for serving up meals

fridge is situated beneath central part of food preparation area

sink is positioned to share natural light with food preparation area, and fitting the sink butted up against the wall leaves a larger continuous food preparation area

eating area is positioned so that as much access as possible is made available, while still being close to the serving area

door can be opened without danger of knocking into anyone working in the kitchen

fitted kitchens

The term 'fitted kitchen' is used to describe a type of kitchen where the units are fixed in place to create the impression they are built into the room, and the majority of modern kitchens are of the 'fitted' variety. Naturally, the appearance and function of individual units will vary between manufacturers, but all units can be categorized according to whether they are handmade or standard, and whether they are fixed to the floor or attached to the wall above a worktop.

handmade units

Handmade items are traditionally more expensive than standard items, as the labour costs are greater and the materials used tend to be of higher quality – kitchen units are no exception to this rule. All the doors, drawers and carcasses of handmade units are constructed using traditional jointing methods, such as dovetail jointing, and tend to be made from solid soft- or hardwoods, which guarantees durability, rather than particle board and laminate. Fitting handmade kitchens is a highly specialized job and most people do not attempt to undertake it themselves.

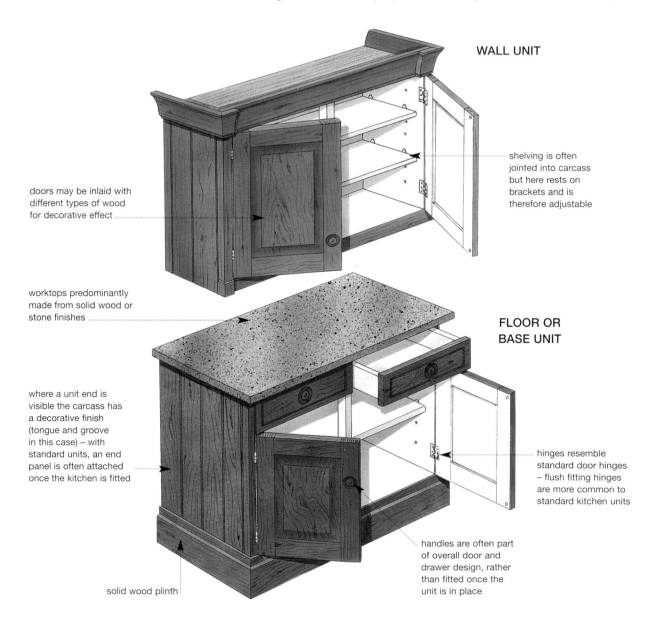

WALL UNIT

shelving is often jointed into carcass but here rests on brackets and is therefore adjustable

doors may be inlaid with different types of wood for decorative effect

worktops predominantly made from solid wood or stone finishes

FLOOR OR BASE UNIT

where a unit end is visible the carcass has a decorative finish (tongue and groove in this case) – with standard units, an end panel is often attached once the kitchen is fitted

hinges resemble standard door hinges – flush fitting hinges are more common to standard kitchen units

solid wood plinth

handles are often part of overall door and drawer design, rather than fitted once the unit is in place

Standard kitchen units are much cheaper than handmade varieties because they are mass-produced and usually made from particle board with a laminate finish, although quality and price do vary considerably. As well as aiming to achieve a pleasing appearance, modern designs are increasingly geared towards specific needs in the kitchen.

self-assembly

Commonly known as 'flat-pack', self- assembly units are supplied broken down into their constituent parts, and, as their name suggests, it is up to the individual to put them together. Self-assembly units occupy the lower end of the price scale, but there are some exceptionally good quality units available and by choosing carefully you can produce a very fine kitchen. Greater time will be needed for installation, but this can be set against the financial gains.

rigid

The main difference between rigid units and flat-packs is that rigid units are supplied factory assembled to reduce the time for installation. As a rule, however, only the carcass is supplied ready-made and you will still need to fit doors, drawer fronts and other accessories. This allows the manufacturer to supply general carcass units that can be adpated to suit the finished look of a kitchen. Different carcasses are discussed in greater detail on pages 26–7.

combination

Combination units are supplied semi-assembled, so that part of the unit may be considered rigid, while the other part is in effect self-assembly. Corner units and carousels are often combination, as well as carcasses that are used to house accessories such as fridges or ovens. By being semi-assembled these carcasses can be adapted to fit different types of accessories and to house a greater variety of appliances, offering more choice to the customer.

fitted kitchens

15

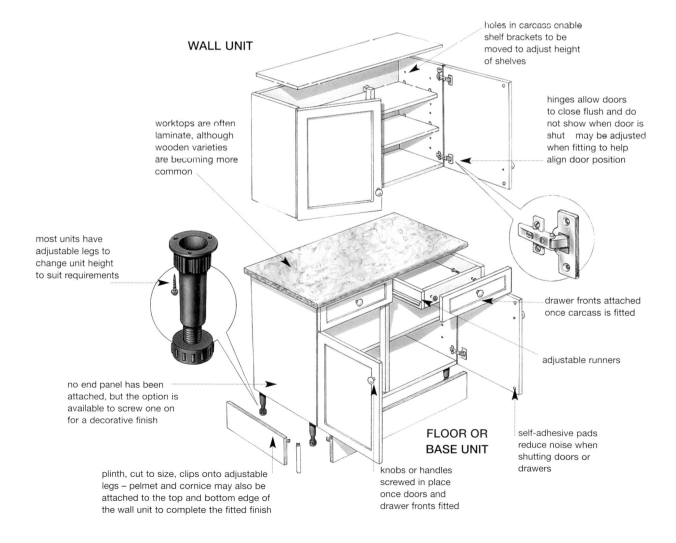

WALL UNIT

holes in carcass enable shelf brackets to be moved to adjust height of shelves

hinges allow doors to close flush and do not show when door is shut — may be adjusted when fitting to help align door position

worktops are often laminate, although wooden varieties are becoming more common

most units have adjustable legs to change unit height to suit requirements

drawer fronts attached once carcass is fitted

adjustable runners

no end panel has been attached, but the option is available to screw one on for a decorative finish

FLOOR OR BASE UNIT

self-adhesive pads reduce noise when shutting doors or drawers

plinth, cut to size, clips onto adjustable legs – pelmet and cornice may also be attached to the top and bottom edge of the wall unit to complete the fitted finish

knobs or handles screwed in place once doors and drawer fronts fitted

unfitted kitchens

Unfitted kitchens offer a more traditional look since they refer back to an era when kitchen furniture and worktops were separate items not permanently fixed to walls or ceilings, with individual dressers and sideboards comprising the main utility items in the kitchen in addition to sink units. The unfitted look has enjoyed something of a revival with many manufacturers now offering semi-fitted ranges that imitate this type of traditional kitchen design.

free-standing units

The main visible difference between free-standing units and standard kitchen units is that the former tend to resemble more closely the look of everyday furniture found elsewhere in the house. Thus a storage unit may have a closer connection in terms of appearance to a wardrobe or cabinet than to modern base and wall units. However, the actual way in which free-standing units are now constructed and fitted is similar to that of standard kitchen units. For example, the doors and drawers in free-standing units will have been constructed using exactly the same method as their 'fitted' counterparts, even though the sizes may be slightly more unusual, and they will still need to be attached to the unit carcass once it is in place. The diagram below provides an example of a free-standing unit and also points out the various features it shares with a standard kitchen unit.

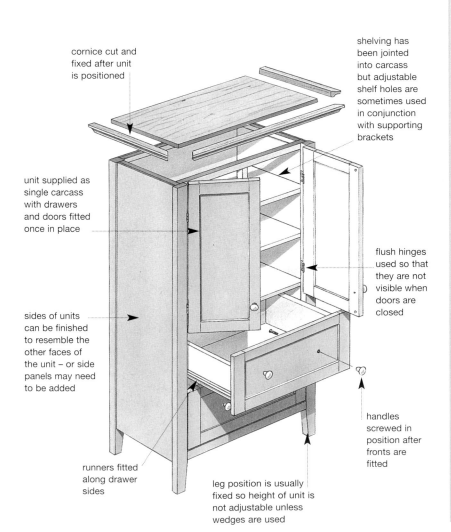

cornice cut and fixed after unit is positioned

shelving has been jointed into carcass but adjustable shelf holes are sometimes used in conjunction with supporting brackets

unit supplied as single carcass with drawers and doors fitted once in place

flush hinges used so that they are not visible when doors are closed

sides of units can be finished to resemble the other faces of the unit – or side panels may need to be added

runners fitted along drawer sides

leg position is usually fixed so height of unit is not adjustable unless wedges are used

handles screwed in position after fronts are fitted

ACCESSORY UNITS

It is also possible to purchase free-standing accessory units, such as units for holding sinks, although it is likely that the unit will be supplied still requiring a substantial amount of assembly and the worktop will also require cutting to fit the sink. Thus although the unfitted look is now being catered for by manufacturers, it must be understood that there will still be a fair amount of fitting and assembling in order to achieve the finished unit look.

TRADITIONAL IDEAS

It is also possible to achieve an unfitted look by using more traditional pieces of furniture such as sideboards or dressers. New reproductions may be purchased or older items can be decorated to meet your preferences. This is an attractive option when producing a 'distressed' paint effect, as older items lend themselves well to creating this type of look. Also consider combining new units with old to create a more haphazard look, which can still provide a pleasing design.

Provided that access is not hindered, positioning an island unit in the central floor area of a kitchen is a sensible use of space. The simple kitchen table represents the most traditional and basic form of island unit, and this type has always been popular due to the variety of functions it can fulfil – acting equally well as a food preparation area, a dining area and more often than not an activity area for the whole family. The only difference with modern kitchens is that a greater choice of designs is now available, with additions being made to enhance utility and the aesthetic appeal. Island units usually do not need to be fixed in place owing to their weight, which means that they are also still moveable. The diagram below shows a typical island unit that incorporates a hanging rack to provide a further storage area in what would otherwise simply be redundant ceiling space.

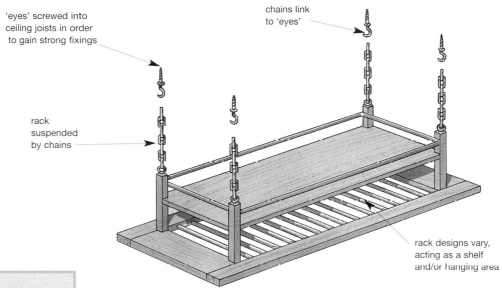

'eyes' screwed into ceiling joists in order to gain strong fixings

chains link to 'eyes'

rack suspended by chains

rack designs vary, acting as a shelf and/or hanging area

safety advice

When deciding on the position for hanging racks it is important to use a joist and cable detector. This will ensure that fixings are inserted into joists to provide adequate support, while avoiding any cables or pipes that run across the ceiling space.

ALTERNATIVE ISLANDS

Standard kitchen units can also be used to create islands in the centre of a room. These are fixed in place and have the characteristics of standard unit design. It is also possible to fit sinks or cooking areas into island units, but this will require water or gas and/or electrical supplies to be fed to these areas, which can be a tricky job. However, in the right size of kitchen the effect of such units can be well worth the work involved.

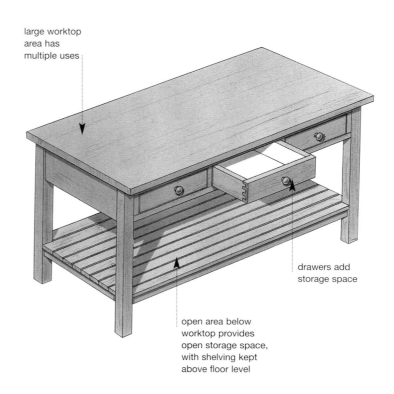

large worktop area has multiple uses

drawers add storage space

open area below worktop provides open storage space, with shelving kept above floor level

how kitchens are installed

The job of fitting a kitchen can be divided into visible and unseen elements. The most important visible elements are the units and various integrating items, such as worktop, plinth and doors and drawer fronts, that combine to make up a fitted 'run'. The unseen part of fitting a kitchen involves routing the water supply, waste disposal, electrics and gas (if required) so that all the working elements function properly and any unsightly pipes are concealed from view.

units

A fitted kitchen is constructed from a number of units, joined together and fixed in place in one or more continuous runs in order to create an integrated or built-in look. In this way the final appearance of the kitchen conceals the constituent parts. The diagram below helps to show how the various units interact to create the finished fitted kitchen.

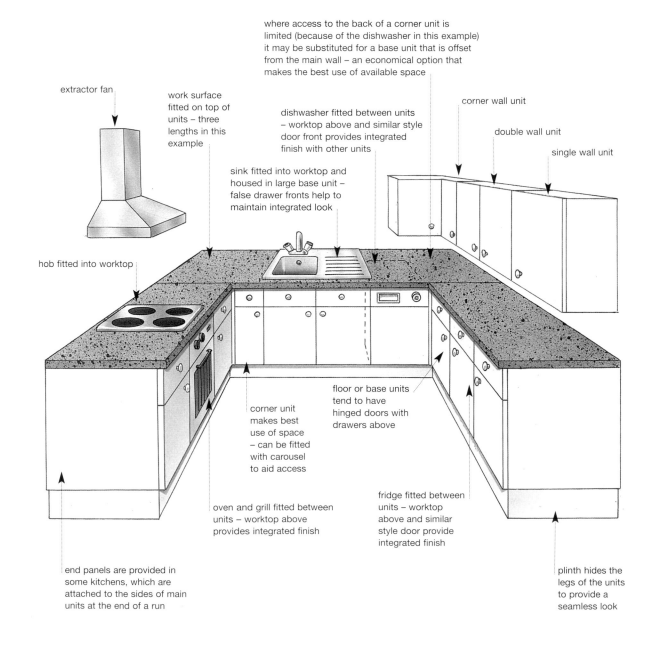

where access to the back of a corner unit is limited (because of the dishwasher in this example) it may be substituted for a base unit that is offset from the main wall – an economical option that makes the best use of available space

extractor fan

work surface fitted on top of units – three lengths in this example

dishwasher fitted between units – worktop above and similar style door front provides integrated finish with other units

corner wall unit

double wall unit

single wall unit

sink fitted into worktop and housed in large base unit – false drawer fronts help to maintain integrated look

hob fitted into worktop

corner unit makes best use of space – can be fitted with carousel to aid access

floor or base units tend to have hinged doors with drawers above

oven and grill fitted between units – worktop above provides integrated finish

fridge fitted between units – worktop above and similar style door provide integrated finish

end panels are provided in some kitchens, which are attached to the sides of main units at the end of a run

plinth hides the legs of the units to provide a seamless look

plumbing & gas

The plumbing system in a fitted kitchen, comprising hot and cold water supplies and waste disposal, should as far as possible be concealed by the unit design, and if the cooker uses gas then the gas supply pipe will be another unseen element. The diagram below shows how plumbing and gas services may be routed in a simple kitchen design.

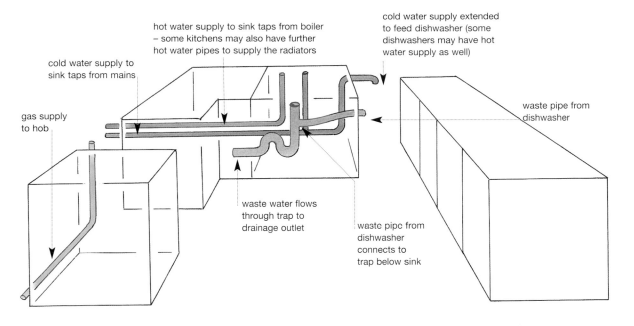

hot water supply to sink taps from boiler – some kitchens may also have further hot water pipes to supply the radiators

cold water supply extended to feed dishwasher (some dishwashers may have hot water supply as well)

cold water supply to sink taps from mains

waste pipe from dishwasher

gas supply to hob

waste water flows through trap to drainage outlet

waste pipe from dishwasher connects to trap below sink

electrics

The electrical supply is another key unseen element in a kitchen. The complexity of this supply can often be underestimated and it can be surprising to find that so many cables are needed. The diagram below illustrates the different electrical needs for a fully functioning kitchen and demonstrates the ideal layout of all the cables.

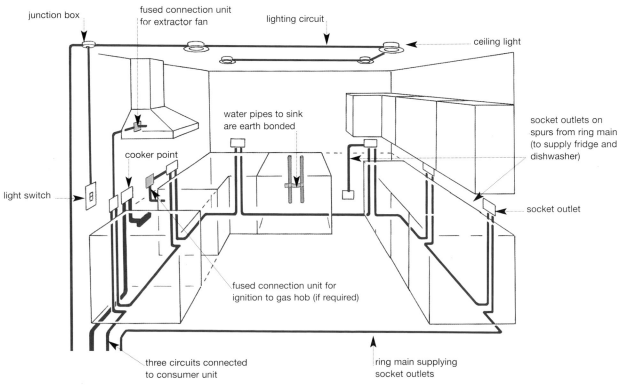

junction box

fused connection unit for extractor fan

lighting circuit

ceiling light

water pipes to sink are earth bonded

socket outlets on spurs from ring main (to supply fridge and dishwasher)

cooker point

light switch

socket outlet

fused connection unit for ignition to gas hob (if required)

three circuits connected to consumer unit

ring main supplying socket outlets

planning

Planning to carry out work on a kitchen is a complicated procedure. Many different skills and techniques are involved in the process of fitting and finishing, and to achieve a successful renovation it is essential to coordinate the timing and order of work for particular tasks. Choices must be made concerning the types of units and accessories you require. You must decide how much of the fitting procedure you intend to carry out yourself and how much will need to be undertaken by a professional tradesperson. It is therefore important to take some time in the planning procedure to avoid making mistakes that may be difficult to rectify once work is underway. This chapter outlines all these issues and offers guidance to help you prepare for the tasks ahead.

The awkward shape of this kitchen and the need to incorporate an eating area has required careful planning.

options for change

The style chosen for a kitchen ulitmately comes down to personal taste but it is always important to be aware of the options available to buy. You may discover that your intial aspirations will need to be cast aside – usually for the best – once you have undertaken a little research into the choices offered by the market place. The most important choice is obviously the style of units, since these will provide the key-note look to the room, but you should also consider carefully how floor, wall and worktop finishes will complement the units to best achieve the desired effect. Nor must it be forgotten that a kitchen is above all a functional space with practical demands.

contemporary

A contemporary-style kitchen design will take into account current fashions and influences, concentrating both on creating a modern appearance and incorporating improved design initiatives that will add to overall utility and efficient functioning of the room. In addition to the fitted units, accessories such as extractor fans can play an important role to ensure that all your needs are catered for. There will be wide variation of cost in this area, and it is important to gain the best value for money from your investment.

RIGHT *Contrasting the neutral tones of the units and worktop with vibrantly coloured walls produces a comfortable feel and adds character to this modern kitchen design.*

ultra-modern

Modern design can be taken a stage further to produce kitchens with an almost futuristic feel. Areas such as tap or handle design, and other furnishings, play a vital role in producing this look, which seeks to create a completely individual and unique appearance. Ultra-modern kitchens will often fall into the higher end of the pricing scale, but more and more manufacturers are producing such designs for people with less extravagant budgets.

LEFT *Stainless steel and aluminium have become the hallmarks of futuristic style, with man-made plastics and laminates often used to complement these finishes – the prominent pole and stylish chairs of the breakfast bar complete the space age look.*

rustic

The rustic look draws upon the charm and wholesome simplicity of country life and is always a popular choice of kitchen design, even if the home is not in particularly rural surroundings. Features such as tiled worktops and hard tile or flagstone floors will further enhance the rustic feel of the units, providing a very homely kitchen environment – though not especially comfortable underfoot. A rustic feel is often synonymous with past times, and to create a consistent effect you may also need to think about methods of concealing modern appliances.

classic

The classic kitchen style derives from the early period of fitted kitchen design and in many ways is difficult to categorize. Some key characteristics, however, are simplicity in design, with base units and wall units in similar proportions and natural wood finishes.

ABOVE RIGHT *A large cooker and hob accentuates the rustic feel of this kitchen, where the wooden unit fronts help to provide a natural yet elegant appearance.*

MIDDLE RIGHT *Simple unit design and decoration produces a very practical kitchen that can still provide a highly attractive, classic-style finish.*

BELOW *Fitted wooden worktop blends well with dressers or pine dining tables, helping to integrate the fitted kitchen look with the more traditional unfitted approach.*

combination

Not all kitchens need comprise entirely of fitted elements and a run of units is often well complemented by a separate piece of furniture. In many cases, combining the fitted with the unfitted look provides the opportunity to apply your own finishing touches to create a more individual look. Open-plan kitchens, where space is not restricted, tend to suit this look the best.

planning a kitchen

A vital part of the planning process is to formulate a detailed diagram of the room with all dimensions indicated. Taking accurate measurements will be crucial for effective installation in the future, and it is a good idea to check measurements several times over. If you are planning for a new home, however, you may find it difficult to gain access to the property. Most people will allow one or two visits to help with your planning, but if this is impossible it is best not to trust the estate agent's dimensions as these will generally be approximate figures.

measuring up a room

The diagram below provides a good example of a basic room design. Although simple in shape, a surprisingly large amount of measurements will need to be taken for accurate planning purposes. As well as noting the physical dimensions of the room, it is also worth taking into account the positions of electrical sockets and water and/or gas supply pipes, which will play an important part in deciding the layout of the kitchen (see also pages 18–19).

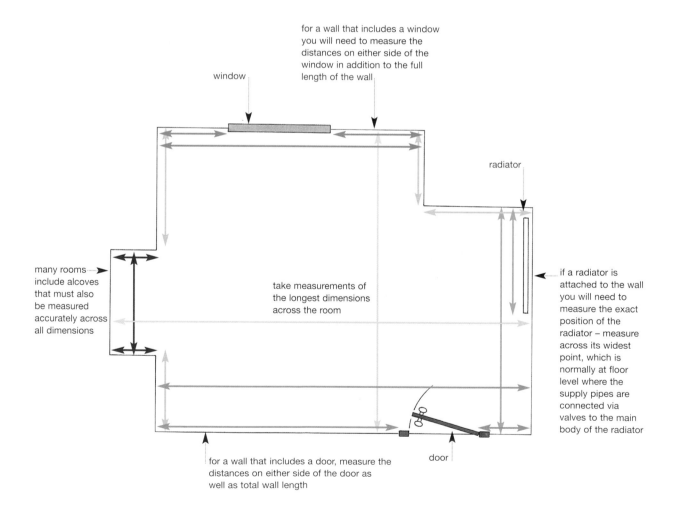

for a wall that includes a window you will need to measure the distances on either side of the window in addition to the full length of the wall

window

radiator

many rooms include alcoves that must also be measured accurately across all dimensions

take measurements of the longest dimensions across the room

if a radiator is attached to the wall you will need to measure the exact position of the radiator – measure across its widest point, which is normally at floor level where the supply pipes are connected via valves to the main body of the radiator

for a wall that includes a door, measure the distances on either side of the door as well as total wall length

door

other considerations

Aside from dimension measurements, a checklist of other items will need to be to taken into account. Below are examples of just some of the many questions that should be asked when planning the layout of a kitchen, but the list is by no means exhaustive and each room will have its own specific characteristics that will need to be addressed.

- What is the height of the room? Will all sizes of wall unit fit comfortably below ceiling level?
- Is the room too narrow to accommodate units on opposing walls?
- Are there any beams or other immovable obstacles that will upset the run of wall units or base units?
- Is there a picture rail that will need moving to make way for wall units?
- Is the floor sloping such that it may create problems with levelling units?
- Is the floor concrete? If so, you cannot run cables or supplies underneath.

- Is the floor constructed from floorboards? If so, this will allow easy access to reroute pipes and cables.
- Is the room split level? Are the two areas joined by steps?
- Does the main door in the room open in or out?
- Are there any attractive features, such as arches or small alcoves, that may be incorporated in the new kitchen design?
- Do the measurements I have made on either side of the door take into account the architrave?

- Are there any meter units (for example, gas or electric) that will either need to be moved or incorporated into units?
- Are there any stopcocks in the room?
- Is there a ducted extraction system for the cooker and will this remain in the same position?
- What is the height of the window sills? Will this cause a problem when fitting worktops below them?
- Will it still be possible to open and close the window easily if a worktop is fitted in front of it?

unit and accessory size

Kitchen manufacturers try to make units and accessories in standard sizes to facilitate the planning process. For example, base units tend to range in width from 100cm (3ft 3in) to 30cm (1ft). Wall units are generally shallower in depth than base units, which are normally manufactured to the same depth as appliances such as cookers and fridges, to achieve the fitted look. When making a scale plan, use the specific measurements for your chosen design of units. Also be aware that some appliances are designed to be fitted with specific units and cross-matching can cause problems.

making a plan

When you come to transfer the measurements onto a scale diagram of the kitchen, the importance of accuracy will become self-evident. The plan you make must take into account all the questions and considerations discussed on these pages, as well as the points covered in establishing the general shape of a kitchen on pages 12–13. Graph paper will help to form a good overhead plan of the kitchen design. If you take your measurements to a kitchen manufacturer they will be able to produce a more detailed plan that will include side elevations. This stage of planning must be linked with the job of choosing units and appliances, discussed in the rest of this chapter.

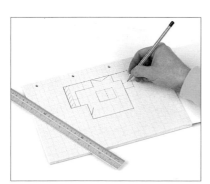

Formulate a scale overhead plan of your kitchen design using graph paper.

Manufacturers can produce computer-generated images of your design.

tips of the trade

Although it is vital to produce accurate measurements, fitted kitchens will always have slight tolerances that allow for small adjustments at the fitting stage. For example, infill panels can be supplied to cover small gaps at the end of a run of units, where the dimensions of the wall do not allow for an exact fit. It is better to leave a slight gap that can easily be covered over with an infill panel than to trim down a unit that is too large for the gap.

choosing units

Kitchen units can be divided up into two basic categories: base or floor units and wall units – most fitted kitchen layouts are designed with base and wall units as a starting point. You will find, however, that there is great variation within each category. For example, peninsula storage is considered to be a type of wall unit even though it extends out into the room like base units and is fixed to a system of support rails and posts rather than the wall.

base units

Sometimes also called floor units, the category of base units can be further sub-divided according to whether or not drawer storage is included. Units that do not feature

drawers are called 'highline' and those that do are referred to as 'drawer line'. There is considerable variation in design and a few such examples are provided below.

large highline base unit

large drawer line base unit

wine rack base unit

three drawer base unit

small drawer line base unit

self-assembly section
for carousel base unit

carousel shelf

carousel base unit

As their name suggests, wall units are hung on the wall and act as storage areas above the worktop. They are slightly shallower in depth than base units to allow access to the worktop area below for food preparation. Wall units are supplied in numerous styles, shapes and widths to suit a variety of storage needs and to account for such obstacles as corners and height requirement above hobs (see page 52). Below are a few examples of wall unit design.

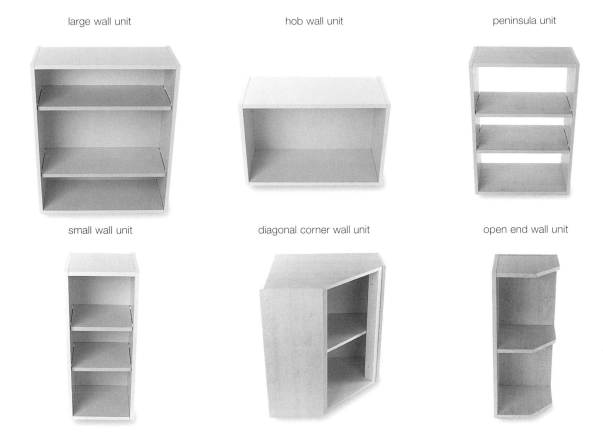

large wall unit   hob wall unit   peninsula unit

small wall unit   diagonal corner wall unit   open end wall unit

trims & accessories

Aside from the carcasses (the basic frame of the units), various trims and accessories are also required to finish the look of the units – most notably drawer fronts and doors, which tend to provide the finished look of the kitchen. However there are many other elements needed to fix units together and to provide the fitted appearance to a run.

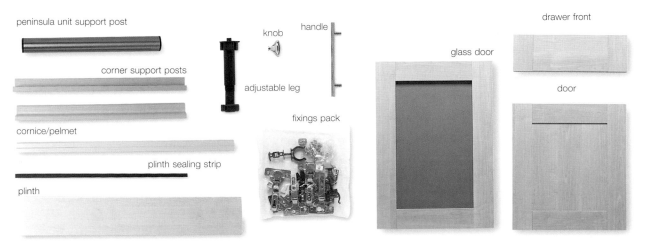

peninsula unit support post

corner support posts

cornice/pelmet

plinth sealing strip

plinth

knob

handle

adjustable leg

fixings pack

glass door

drawer front

door

choosing a worktop

Of all the areas in a kitchen, the worktop arguably suffers the greatest wear and tear. Daily food preparation and frequent spillages cause the worktop to be constantly worn and wiped down, and as such it needs to be constructed from materials that can withstand this form of regular abrasion. Both natural and man-made finishes are available and there is a tendency for the latter to mimic the look of natural finishes.

Worktops are often chosen to contrast with the finish of the units, in order to provide a clean dividing line between the two different surfaces. The cost of a worktop will vary dramatically according to the type of material it is made from. Man-made laminates tend to occupy the lower range of the price scale, while solid stone or marble worktops are considerably more expensive. The choice of worktop material will ultimately be determined by your available budget, but it is always worth remembering that a cheaper worktop will often wear out more quickly, causing greater expense in the long term when they need to be replaced.

laminate

Laminate worktop is generally constructed from a particle board base with a laminated plastic layer stuck to the board to provide the finished effect. It is quite durable and easy to keep spotlessly clean. Colours and designs are hugely varied and competitive pricing makes laminate worktop a popular choice.

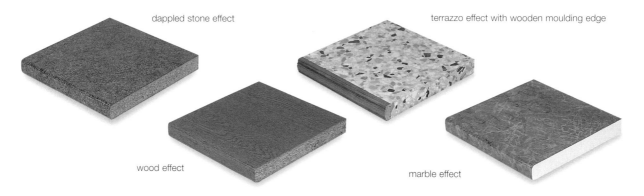

dappled stone effect

terrazzo effect with wooden moulding edge

wood effect

marble effect

wood

Wooden worktop represents the classical choice for fitted kitchens and is more popular now than ever before. The cost will vary according to the type of wood used, but it is normally possible to choose a wooden worktop on even a limited budget. Although this type of worktop is often categorized as solid wood, many are in fact made up of strips or blocks that have been glued together to provide a solid structure.

cherry

light oak

dark oak

beech block

synthetic stone

Synthetic stone worktop is formed from a blend of natural minerals and clear acrylic. It provides a very hardwearing finish and, as the name suggests, produces a perfect representation of a decorative stone finish. Whereas laminate and wooden worktops are supplied as standard lengths, synthetic stone worktop must be ordered to size and is generally shaped and formed by the manufacturer to deal with your precise requirements.

slate effect

granite effect

light granite effect

onyx effect

natural stone

Not surprisingly, in most situations a natural stone worktop will exhibit the most hardwearing properties of all worktops, though this durability is reflected in the price and natural stone is certainly not a budget choice. Natural stone is also an aesthetically pleasing option, tying in beautifully with anything from a rustic-looking traditional kitchen to a modern minimalist design. As with synthetic stone, a natural stone worktop tends to be made to order rather than bought in standard lengths, and fitting is almost invariably a job for a professional tradesperson.

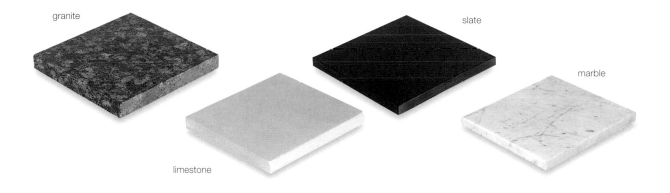

granite

slate

marble

limestone

USING TILES

An alternative to fitting a solid worktop is to create one composed of tiles. When choosing your tiles make sure the manufacturer has recommended them for use as a worktop surface. To the right are a few examples of worktop tiles. For full instructions on how to achieve a tiled worktop, see pages 106–7.

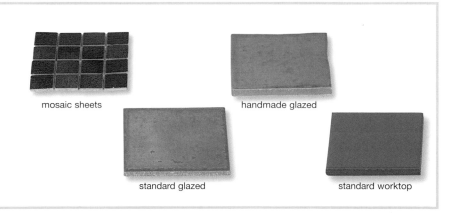

mosaic sheets

handmade glazed

standard glazed

standard worktop

choosing appliances & accessories

An attractive kitchen design is only of practical use if the various appliances and accessories have been chosen carefully to deal with your everyday needs. Most manufacturers will steer you towards those appliances guaranteed to be compatible with their unit design in terms of fitting procedures. For free-standing fridges or cookers this is not so important, but if appliances are to be integrated into a run of units you must ensure the dimensions will fit.

washing appliances

All kitchens need to be fitted with sinks, but it does not follow that all kitchens will contain dishwashers and/or washing machines. Sleek and easily cleaned, stainless steel sink drainers are a popular choice today, although the traditional look of Belfast sinks have become a popular addition to some styles of kitchen. Waste disposal units can be fitted as an extra accessory to most sink designs. Early dishwashers tended to be free-standing, but today it is common to fit integral appliances that do not disrupt the fitted look.

integral dishwasher

stainless steel sink with drainer and central bowl

Belfast sink

taps & connectors

Sinks do not usually come supplied with taps – these will need to be chosen separately – and the range of styles is vast. The key practical issue when making your choice is to ensure the number of inlets for the taps corresponds to the pre-drilled holes in the sink unit. If you have chosen a Belfast sink this should not be a problem as the taps tend to be cut into the worktop. For pre-moulded varieties, however, make sure the taps are compatible. You will also need connectors for joining the taps to the water supply. Flexible tap connectors are ideal but again, check compatibility with the taps and your supply pipe layout.

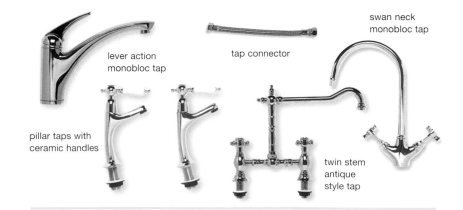

lever action monobloc tap

tap connector

swan neck monobloc tap

pillar taps with ceramic handles

twin stem antique style tap

WATER SOFTENERS

The type of water piped into the house has become an area of concern with many homeowners. If you know that the house is supplied with hard water then it can be worth planning at this early stage to have a water softener installed, which will help to prevent limescale furring.

cooking appliances

The number and size of cooking appliances that you choose to fit in the kitchen will depend upon factors such as family size, general eating habits and how keen you are about cooking as a hobby. As with washing appliances, there is a choice in terms of the free-standing or integrated options. Integral hobs are generally cut into the worktop, and integral ovens are either housed in purpose-made units or slotted into customized gaps in the unit run.

chimney and hood
(extractor fan)

integral gas hob

integral oven

integral electric hob

microwave oven

chilled storage

Although it is possible to fit fridges and freezers into a bank of units, the free-standing varieties have remained more popular. This may be due to practical storage issues, as fridges fitted under a worktop tend to be rather small.

free-standing fridge/freezer

recycling areas

Environmental issues have never been more important and recycling has become a part of everyday life for more and more households. To aid the job of recycling, manufacturers now produce special drawers or bins that can be fitted into kitchen units to provide a ready-made recycling area. There is no excuse not to do your bit!

This recycling bin fits neatly into a standard unit and is automatically accessed when the door is opened. It is divided into two sections to aid the separation of materials.

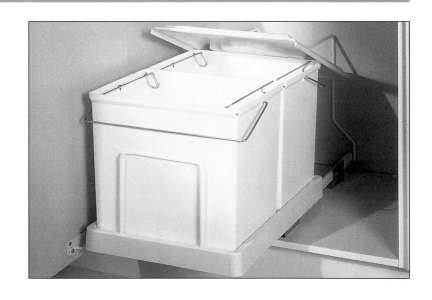

eating areas

When planning your kitchen layout one crucial issue is whether to include an eating area in the design. Space is obviously the most important determining factor but you will generally find most kitchens these days include some sort of eating area. With our busy modern lifestyles it is not uncommon to rush breakfast, grab a quick lunch and have a TV dinner in the evening. A small eating area in the kitchen can encourage people to enjoy, however briefly, a sit-down meal precisely because it offers a much less formal environment for eating than a dining room.

table dining

Combining the kitchen with a dining area may be a necessity if there is no space in your home for a separate dining room, but there are many other reasons to choose to fit a kitchen diner – it can free up the dining room for other purposes, serving up becomes an easier task, and the open-plan design can create a more social atmosphere than with smaller, divided rooms. Manufacturers have developed numerous space-saving options that make it possible to build an effective dining area in even the smallest kitchen.

RIGHT *This drawer design has been modified to provide a pull-out dining surface, ideal for kitchens where space is restricted.*

BELOW *This contemporary kitchen includes a free-standing breakfast bar that could equally be used for lunch and dinner.*

With many fitted kitchen designs, the worktop can be adjusted or extended to produce a multi-purpose area that can be used both for food preparation and as an eating area. Sometimes referred to as breakfast bars, these areas are becoming increasingly popular in modern kitchens. Often the bar will be installed at worktop level, but this can be adjusted to provide a lower surface that is more practical for eating purposes.

RIGHT *Although lower than the rest of the worktop, the surface of this breakfast bar may still also be used to prepare food.*

BELOW *Cut to a curved shape, this worktop has been extended out from a short run of peninsula units to create a handy eating area, which is supported by a metal post.*

Continuing a peninsula unit is another way of using worktop to create an eating area. Lowering the bar gives the illusion of a normal dining table, but its proximity to the main worktop area facilitates its use for food preparation and other worktop activities.

Another option for providing a breakfast bar is to incorporate it into an island unit. One side of the unit can be used to access storage, while the overlap of the worktop on the other side provides an ideal eating area.

BELOW *An over-sized and specially-shaped piece of worktop has been fixed to an island unit so that it hangs over the side opposite the main cooking area, creating a stylish breakfast bar.*

eating areas

33

BREAKFAST BAR OPTIONS

• **Dimensions** – The width of most breakfast bars tends to be larger than standard worktop dimensions to allow people to sit comfortably when eating. Be aware of this size difference when ordering to ensure that the correct size worktop is supplied.

• **Foldaway bars** – In particularly small kitchens where space is at a premium, breakfast bars can be adjusted to allow them to be folded away when not in use. The bar will be hinged along the wall edge so that it may be lifted up into a position flush with the wall surface.

• **Extra furniture** – Remember that some sort of seating arrangement will be required for a breakfast bar. Stools are ideal for worktop level bars, and many kitchen manufacturers now produce designs that will complement the finish of your chosen fitted kitchen.

order of work

Carrying out any home improvement project requires a sensible order of work so that tasks may be completed as quickly and efficiently as possible but always to the highest standard. The kitchen is a room that is in frequent use every day, and as such it is even more important to plan events so that the least possible disruption is caused. A number of factors must be considered to ensure a smooth course is followed throughout the renovation procedure.

budgeting

Buying new kitchen units and accessories is generally a straightforward purchase to budget for as the manufacturer will provide a fixed price. However, on top of this basic cost you will need to account for all the extras detailed below, which can substantially inflate the budget:

- hiring professional tradespeople e.g. for connecting and disconnecting plumbing, electrics and gas
- redecorating the room
- laying new flooring material
- any structural work to be undertaken for larger renovation jobs e.g. changing the position of a wall, or knocking two rooms into one to create an open-plan kitchen diner
- commissioning architectural drawings if carrying out substantial construction work causing structural change
- add a further 10-15% on top of your final figure to account for any unforeseen changes or problems encountered once the work has begun

schedule of work

From start to finish, kitchen installation can take longer than you may first have thought. However, as long as water supplies are not cut for any long period of time, and cooking appliances are changed over in the same day, the kitchen can still be used for essential tasks so that the household will continue to function during this period of upheaval. For planning purposes it is important to have an accurate idea of the timescale for the entire kitchen renovation project. The following factors must be taken into account when drawing up a schedule of work:

- manufacturers will not be able to deliver all the units and accessories the day after you have ordered them – on large projects where a whole kitchen is to be fitted, it is unlikely that the time between order and delivery will be less than four weeks
- most manufacturers will be able to give a rough guide on the time it will take to install the kitchen, but it is always worth adding extra days on top to account for any problems.
- once delivered most new kitchens can be fitted in a week, but the time taken will clearly depend on size and how complicated the layout of the kitchen is
- plan for two to three days preparation prior to delivery (more if building work is required)
- plan for a week after the installation for laying the floor and general decoration
- tradespeople will need to be factored into the schedule – it is likely that plumbers or electricians will need to visit twice, once to adjust connections on the old kitchen (for this you will first need to have undertaken some preparatory work in order to reroute supplies) and once to reconnect when the new one is fitted – coordinate the timing of your work so that they may be booked in advance for the slots you require
- waste disposal is a job that is often overlooked but must also be accounted for in the schedule of work e.g. a skip will probably need to be hired to take all the bits and pieces that comprised the the old kitchen away and you will need to dispose of the packaging used for the new kitchen

dealing with professionals

Decisions will need to be made concerning the extent of the work that you intend and are able to carry out yourself, and the areas where professional help may be required. At some stage it is likely that you will need to contact plumbers or electricians for specific jobs. Bear in mind the following guidelines when hiring professionals and negotiating a price for the work:

- when choosing tradesperson, always get a personal recommendation – scanning classified advertisements for any type of tradesperson is a sure recipe for disaster and should always be avoided
- when looking at the cost for work to be carried out, the figure should not change unless you alter specifications for the work
- get a 'price' not an estimate – tradespeople who produce 'estimates' or 'quotations' should be viewed with some caution as the vagueness of the term allows scope for boosting the bill at the end of the job, whereas an initial 'price' provides good grounds for understanding that this will be the final figure you pay
- never offer to pay tradespeople up front, as this can encourage them to neglect the project – if money is to be paid once work is completed this is a greater incentive for them to stay on site
- if expensive materials need to be bought, however, it is acceptable for the tradesperson to expect that these costs will be met prior to installation
- as mentioned above, tradespeople will usually need to be hired for disconnecting the old kitchen and reconnecting the new – when they offer a quote for the job, make it clear that two visits will be required
- once you have hired a tradesperson, try to get as much advice from them as possible regarding any preparatory work so that their jobs are straightforward when they arrive for work

dealing with manufacturers

Manufacturers will usually only be involved in a kitchen renovation project prior to actual installation, when you are working out the design and choosing styles, although some can also be hired to fit the kitchen. When dealing with a manufacturer to finalize the design of your kitchen, negotiate a price and organize delivery, you will need to consider the following issues:

- ascertain from the start whether your chosen accessories and appliances can be fitted into your design
- as discussed on pages 24–5, it is essential to measure accurately so that a detailed plan may be provided for both you and a manufacturer to decide on the best layout and finish for a new kitchen
- sales representatives are generally well trained and will provide good service, but remember to check for any hidden extras in a kitchen specification and ensure that you are being quoted for all the components that make up the kitchen you desire, e.g. check that plinth, cornice and end panels are included in the price and make sure that handles for doors and drawers are not extra
- most manufacturers will also offer deals, providing free items according to the amount of money you spend – this can obviously be to your advantage, but check that the initial unit price has not been artificially inflated to account for these 'give aways' and ensure that such items are the correct specification for your needs
- if you are employing the kitchen manufacturer to fit the entire kitchen, they will provide a price for the work at the time the kitchen is ordered – this price is normally quite competitive since it forms part of an overall kitchen package, but it can still be worth taking the specifications of your new kitchen to an independent trader and see what price they are prepared to offer
- once a deal has been done, confirm a delivery date – it is rarely possible to buy kitchens 'off the shelf' and there is normally a time delay between the purchase and actual delivery of units and accessories
- when the units and accessories are delivered, you will be surprised by the amount of pieces that are supplied for a fitted kitchen – check and double-check the delivery to ensure that everything has arrived and, most importantly, that no items are damaged, so that you can immediately report back to the manufacturer

tools & materials

A basic tool kit is essential for home improvement work. This needs to contain general construction and multi-purpose tools appropriate for a number of tasks around the home. For dealing specifically with kitchens, this tool kit will need to include items more directly related to a kitchen environment. Some particular building materials may also need to be purchased.

general tools

When assembling a household tool kit, the need for such items as hammers, screwdrivers and saws is fairly evident. There are other tools, however, the use for which may not be so instantly recognizable that are nonetheless essential items. The tools shown in this section will provide a good basis for any household tool kit.

claw hammer

bradawl

nail punch

pipe, joist and cable detector

slot-head screwdrivers

cross head screwdrivers

insulated sleeves

club hammer

bolster chisel

combination pliers

side cutters

long-nose pliers

half-round rasp

general purpose chisels

cordless drill/driver

mini level

carpenter's pencil

tape measure

sealant dispenser

clamp

combination square

hacksaw

stepladder

pointing trowel

panel saw

craft knife

mitre saw

plastic bucket

workbench

power tools

Aside from a cordless/drill driver, which has become an essential part of any household tool kit, other power tools are becoming more and more popular because of their time-saving capabilities and the fact that they are more competitively priced than in the past. It is therefore worth considering building up a good power tool kit, especially if you plan to do more than the odd piece of home improvement work.

power drill

jigsaw

router

electric sander

HIRING TOOLS

For isolated tasks that may require particularly heavy duty equipment, or tools that are very expensive to buy, hiring is often the best option. This area has become a growing sector of the DIY market, and hire shops are increasingly catering for home repair enthusiasts, as well as more traditional trade customers.

plumbing tools

Pipework may often need adjusting to accommodate new installations in a kitchen. Therefore some basic plumbing tools may be required to carry out such alterations and the items below provide a good basis for a simple plumbing tool kit. Only tackle plumbing tasks if you are certain of the correct procedures and seek professional advice if you have any reservations.

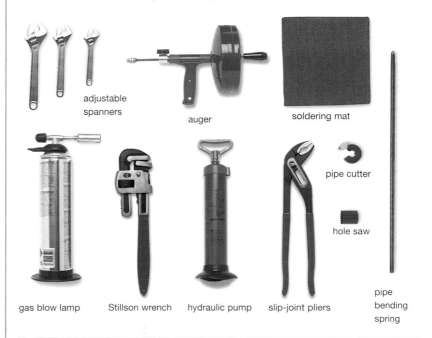

adjustable spanners

auger

soldering mat

pipe cutter

hole saw

gas blow lamp   Stillson wrench   hydraulic pump   slip-joint pliers   pipe bending spring

materials

As well as possessing general purpose tools, it is also important to have access to certain materials that are often required during kitchen repairs or renovations. Some of the items shown below are more specific to plumbing requirements, while others have wider uses in many areas of work within the kitchen.

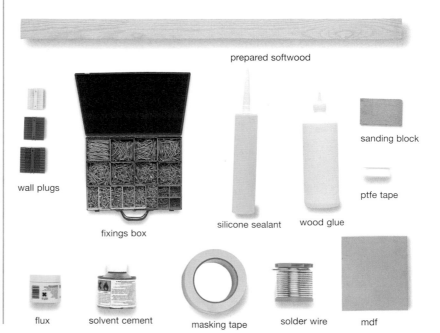

prepared softwood

sanding block

wall plugs

ptfe tape

silicone sealant   wood glue

fixings box

flux   solvent cement   masking tape   solder wire   mdf

fitting kitchen units

To a greater or lesser extent, most modern kitchens are based on a fitted kitchen design that makes the best use of the available space, while still being functional and an attractive addition to the room as a whole. This chapter demonstrates the techniques used for constructing and combining units to produce a fitted kitchen. There are always slight differences in unit design between manufacturers, which means that technique will need to be refined according to those particular needs. However, this chapter helps to demonstrate that most of the general principles involved in fitting a kitchen remain constant, irrespective of manufacturing variations. For those instances where unit design does require a change in technique the different options available are also explained.

This stylish kitchen was constructed by building up carcasses, fitting worktop, attaching fronts and finishing.

preparing the kitchen ↗↗↗

Before installing a new kitchen, it is first necessary to remove any old units and disconnect supplies as required. The extent of the work can vary, but it is generally the case that some units will need to be dismantled, and in nearly all circumstances water supplies will need shutting off.

water & waste

All kitchens have a water supply to the sink, which often divides further to supply a dishwasher and/or washing machine. Before carrying out any work, isolate and shut off the mains supply to these appliances. It may need to be turned off right back at the rising main stopcock, which is usually found close to where the water supply comes into the house or below the kitchen sink, although this is not always the case. It is important to know the location of the stopcock, for both kitchen renovations and in case of emergency. Simply close the tap to turn off the water supply.

✋ safety advice

If you have any doubts about undertaking work on water supplies, always seek professional advice.

tools for the job

slot-head screwdriver

slip-joint pliers

hacksaw or pipe cutter

padsaw

Stillson wrench

adjustable spanners

1 In most modern homes, smaller stopcocks or servicing valves are fitted close to the appliance itself. These may have a handle or can be opened and closed using a slot-head screwdriver. Once the valve is closed, turn on the taps to remove any water remaining between valve and tap.

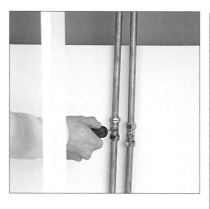

2 Disconnect the waste pipe from the sink. Connections should simply unscrew by hand, but you may need to use slip-joint pliers.

3 Use a hacksaw or pipe cutter to cut through the water supply pipes, at a point well above the servicing valves.

4 Supply pipes are normally integrated into the kitchen unit itself, so take care to avoid damaging the pipes when removing the unit. Remove the front of the unit first, cutting with a padsaw, and leave the back part till last. This allows easier access when you finally cut away the section the pipes are threaded through.

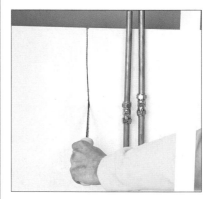

5 Fix a temporary tap to the mains with a Stillson wrench and adjustable spanners.

✋ safety advice

Never carry out work on gas supplies or appliances – employ someone qualified to ensure the fittings are safe. Similarly, seek professional advice when dealing with electrical supplies.

removing units

Removal of kitchen units is a very straightforward task, provided the necessary precautions have been taken and all supplies have been shut down in advance. Most units are connected by a simple system of screws and various designs of jointing block. By undoing these fixings the units can be broken down into smaller sections, making their removal easier. The process of removing an existing kitchen tends to produce a large amount of refuse, which is too bulky to be disposed of along with the household waste. Rather than making several trips to your local tip, therefore, you might want to consider hiring a skip to take away the rubbish.

tools for the job

cordless drill/driver
slot-head screwdriver
cross head screwdriver
club hammer
bolster chisel
protective equipment

1 You will first need to separate the worktop from the units. Most worktops will be attached to units with screw fixings on the underside at both the back and front. Simply unscrew these fixings to remove the worktop.

2 Separate units are often screwed together close to their front edge, with the fixings concealed by small plastic caps for aesthetic purposes. Prise off these caps with a slot-head screwdriver.

3 With the caps out of the way, screws can then be removed in the usual way.

4 You will also most likely need to remove any existing tiles from the walls. Use a club hammer and bolster chisel to knock the old tiles away. (See also pages 118–19 for how to remove tiles.)

(See also pages 118–19 for how to remove tiles.)

safety advice

When using a club hammer and bolster chisel, be sure to wear goggles to protect your eyes from any flying splinters or debris. It is also advisable to wear protective gloves.

GENERAL PREPARATION

Once the old kitchen units are completely removed, you will be in a much better position to determine the extent of making good required before the new kitchen can be fitted. The main areas to consider are:

• **Wallpaper** – Strip all existing wallpaper using a steam stripper if possible, or by soaking and removing the paper with a scraper. A steam stripper is also a useful tool for removing any hardened tile adhesive left on the walls after the tiles have been removed.

• **Plastering** – The messy job of replastering should be carried out at this stage. Remember that in some areas it may not be necessary to extend new plaster below worktop level, since the wall space will be covered by new units.

• **Flooring** – Old flooring should also be removed at this stage, so that new flooring can be laid after the kitchen has been fitted.

tips of the trade

Carry out as much wall and surface preparation as possible before fitting the new kitchen. In this way all the messier jobs will have been done, thereby reducing the risk of damaging the new units. Kitchens tend to be fiddly rooms to decorate, so it can also be worth applying the first coat of wall and ceiling colour prior to fitting the new units. Only one further paint coat will be required once the kitchen is fitted, thus saving a lot of time.

preparing electrics & plumbing ⁄⁄⁄⁄

Extensive plumbing and electrical work are jobs for professional tradespeople, but there is still a great deal of planning required in the positioning of these services. Extensive work will obviously increase costs, so if possible try not to move too many services from their original positions. That said, there is nothing worse than a newly fitted kitchen with lighting and electrical sockets in awkward positions, so it is best not to compromise on efficient design for the sake of less work.

plan for new services

The diagram below shows an example of a design for an average-sized kitchen, and draws attention to the main areas of concern when deciding on service and supply. You need to think carefully about where light sources are positioned and where sockets will go. Most of the points outlined may be related to all types of fitted kitchen.

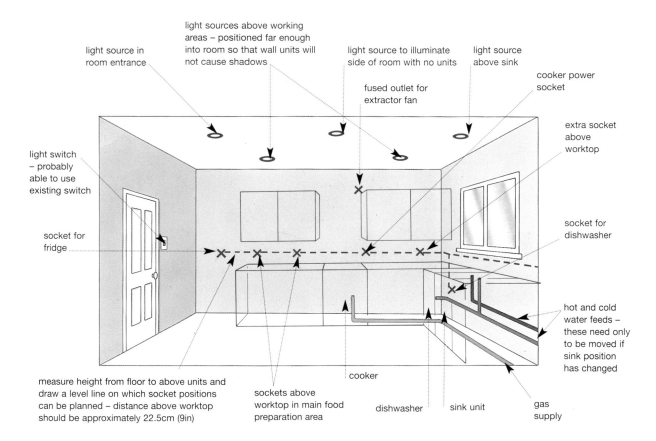

light source in room entrance

light sources above working areas – positioned far enough into room so that wall units will not cause shadows

light source to illuminate side of room with no units

light source above sink

fused outlet for extractor fan

cooker power socket

extra socket above worktop

light switch – probably able to use existing switch

socket for fridge

socket for dishwasher

hot and cold water feeds – these need only to be moved if sink position has changed

measure height from floor to above units and draw a level line on which socket positions can be planned – distance above worktop should be approximately 22.5cm (9in)

sockets above worktop in main food preparation area

cooker

dishwasher

sink unit

gas supply

electric supplies

It is easy to guide cables through the void in hollow walls but you will need to chase out channels in solid walls.

safety advice

Always seek professional advice when dealing with gas or electrical supplies.

tools for the job

pencil & tape measure

safety equipment

power drill

bolster & chisel

1 Draw pencil guidelines on the wall to mark the cable position. Use a club hammer and bolster chisel

to cut through the plaster into the blocks below. Drill holes down each line with a power drill to ease the process. Remove material to a depth of about 2.5cm (1in). Wear gloves and goggles to protect from flying debris.

2 Position the cable in the chased out channel, ensuring that it sits well below surface level.

3 Before plastering over the cable, it is always best to cover it with some impact resistant plastic channel to protect it from wear and tear. This should be held in place with galvanized nails.

WIRING OPTIONS

To achieve a fully-fitted look to a kitchen it is better to hide cables below surface level on walls, but it is possible to have cables running through trunking or conduit on the wall surface. You could combine both techniques so that only wall areas that are in view have hidden cables.

plumbing supplies

Plumbing supply and waste pipes can vary considerably in terms of size and methods for connecting and joining. Copper pipe is still very common for water supply, but it is possible to use other materials such as polybutylene pipe. Waste pipes tend to be pvc based with diameters varying according to specific needs.

compression joints

These are used to join two lengths of copper pipe. The joint itself is a threaded connection unit, which is then tightened onto each length of pipe using spanners rotating the joint nuts in opposing directions. Inside each nut is an 'olive', which tightens onto the copper pipe creating a watertight seal. Compression joints are not particularly attractive, but in kitchen situations they will normally be obscured from view and therefore provide an easy technique for lengthening pipe supply.

soldered joints

This is another, slightly neater method for connecting copper pipe. The joints themselves are supplied as straight, elbow, or in tee connector form so that options are available to change pipe direction and/or extend supply. There are two types of soldered joint: end feed joints, which require solder wire to be applied during the joining

process and integral ring joints, which already have solder inside the joint that will be activated with heat. The latter are clearly easier to use, but more expensive. In either case, the pipe ends to be joined must be completely clean and flux should be applied to the pipe ends to aid this process. In this case, an integral ring joint is used, where a gas torch applies heat to the joint causing the solder to melt inside the pipe and create a watertight seal. Always take care when using gas torches as they are an obvious fire hazard, and use a flameproof mat.

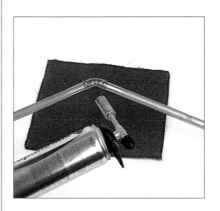

push fit joints

These are used to join plastic waste pipes and offer a very simple connecting method compared to solvent welded plastic joints. It is also worth remembering that, in kitchens, most pipes connecting to the sink can be joined using this technique, or they are threaded and therefore make the jointing process even easier.

assembling flat-pack units

'Flat-pack' is the name given to a unit or carcass that requires assembly before being fitted, so called because of the way they are delivered. Methods for construction will always vary slightly between manufacturers and for different types of unit, but general principles of assembly do remain constant. This chapter demonstrates how to construct a large base unit and covers almost all the techniques you are likely to come across.

There can be a surprising number of components in a flat-pack. It is best to lay out all the unit sections and panels first, then check the fixing pack to ensure you have the correct number of sections and the appropriate choice and quantity of fixings.

tools for the job

slot-head screwdriver

cross head screwdriver

cordless drill/driver

hammer

tips of the trade

It can be worth undertaking one or two dry runs putting the unit together without fixings. This helps to work out how each section relates to the other once the whole unit is complete. Always check each new section has been positioned the right way up.

1 Many flat-packs are assembled following a system of cam studs and screws in pre-drilled holes. This offers an efficient connection as the

holes are drilled with great accuracy in a factory. Position studs according to the guidelines and screw them by hand into the pre-drilled holes. Some studs may need a few turns of the screwdriver to fit securely.

2 Fix drawer runners on the side panels of the unit, following the marked-off positions. Only attach a runner on each side panel if the unit includes two drawers. Choose correct screws for the runners – if they are too long you risk going all the way through and damaging the outer surface.

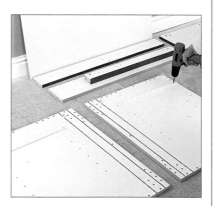

3 Position plastic threaded dowels in pre-drilled holes on the base section and the ends of connecting

sections. These dowels simply push into place and will make joints much stronger when the unit is assembled. Some manufacturers use wooden dowels, which will require gluing (see drawers in step 10).

4 Insert cam screws in the appropriate holes indicated (these will eventually correspond with the holes that have had the cam studs already inserted into them). Again, you should be able just to press these screws into position by hand. Make sure the open side of the cam screw faces the edge of the section, so that it will be possible to join the section to the side panel with the corresponding cam stud. Ensure that the head of the cam screw fits flush with the surrounding panel surface.

5 Use the central strengthening upright as the starting point for full assembly. Connect the base of the upright to the base section, and screw the top strengthening rail in place on top of the upright. Continue to check that each section is being positioned the right way up.

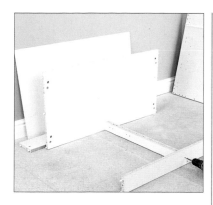

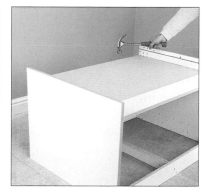

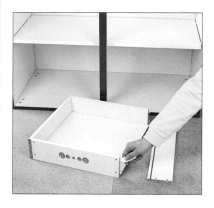

10 Drawers are usually assembled with dowels, often made of wood and therefore require gluing before the drawer unit is fitted together. If no glue is supplied, normal pva will suffice. Wipe away any excess with a cloth before it dries.

6 The side sections of the unit can now be put in place using the position of the dowels, and cam studs and screws, as a guide. Tighten the cam screws to produce a rigid structure. To encourage the cam fixings and dowels to align, you may need to make one or two gentle blows with the butt end of a hammer on the outside of the side sections.

8 Clip the shelf supports in place. These should push in by hand but you may need to apply one or two knocks with the butt end of a hammer. Now insert the central shelf, allowing it to come to rest on the supports. The shelf will either be held in position by the force of gravity or it will have a clip design, resting both below and on top of the shelf to hold it in position.

11 Allow the dowelled joints to dry before fixing runners to the drawer. Screw them in position, perpendicular to the drawer edge.

7 The back panel may now be added. This normally slides into position in purpose-made channels in the side panels. You will find that back panels are more often than not thinner than the other section, since they provide no structural strength to the unit as a whole. Secure them in place by nailing panel pins along the bottom edge of the back panel into the edge of the base section. Ensure that the pins are inserted perpendicular to the base panel edge rather than at an angle – If you make an angled insertion, this can cause the pins to break through the surface of the base panel, which results in a weak fixing and unsightly blemish.

9 Screw the central drawer runner(s) in position. Two central runners will be needed for a unit with two drawers (one either side of the central vertical upright), otherwise only one will be required.

12 Finally position the drawer(s), and the unit is ready for the first stage of the kitchen-fitting process.

getting level ⁊⁊

When installing a new fitted kitchen, it is vital to ensure work begins from a level starting point. From this point the whole kitchen is developed and any inaccuracy at this stage will be magnified as work continues. The importance of taking time to get a level starting point cannot be emphasized enough.

measuring & marking

The aim is to mark a horizontal level guideline at a height corresponding to the top of the base units, which should always be fitted first. If the units are rigid with no feet to allow height adjustment, the guideline will be equal to unit height. Where units have adjustable feet, a good height is 87–9cm (34–5in). To make the guideline you will need to measure up the highest point in the floor level. Not all floors are perfectly 'true' and you will need to make adjustments at this stage to counteract the situation.

tools for the job

spirit level

tape measure

pencil

1 In most kitchens at least one unit will be fitted in or around a corner (see pages 50–1). This makes an ideal starting point and you should try to fix the level guideline from one of the corners. If you have a choice

of corners, take your level line from the highest. If there are no corner units, simply find the highest point along the floor. Lie a long length of batten on the floor, up against the skirting board, then position a spirit level on top to gauge which way the floor is 'running'.

2 Mark off at the desired unit height, measuring from the floor up the wall surface.

3 No further measurements need be taken up the wall surface, but simply use the spirit level to draw a horizontal guideline on the wall. This will represent the height at which the kitchen units will be fitted.

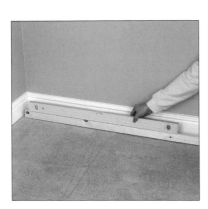

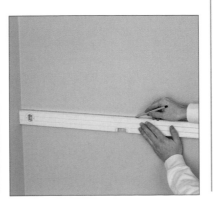

4 Make an accurate plan of the position of units by marking off along the guideline where one unit ends and the next will begin. Refer to your kitchen plan in order to gain accurate measurements.

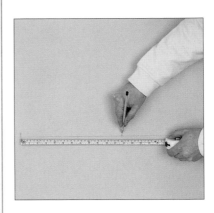

using a batten

Attaching a batten along the level guideline will facilitate the process of fitting units, but is not always specified by manufacturers. However, the batten approach creates an excellent fixing point for units and provides extra support for the worktop once fitted. If the units are not particularly deep, and as such will be set away from the wall, you will definitely need to attach batten to support the worktop. With deeper units personal choice comes into play. Techniques for fixing units to a wall with or without batten are discussed more fully on pages 48–9.

tools for the job

panel saw

cordless drill/drver

power drill

hammer

using concrete anchors

For solid walls, concrete anchors are the ideal choice as they offer by far the quickest method and create exceptionally strong fixings.

safety advice

Before knocking in any fixings, always check the wall surface using a pipe and cable detector.

1 Cut a piece of batten to length, then drill through it directly into the wall surface below. Drill bit size should correspond to that of the concrete anchor screws being used.

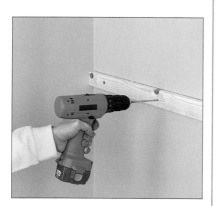

2 To create a solid fixture, simply screw the concrete anchors directly through the batten and into the solid wall below. Continue to make fixings about 30–45cm (12–18in) apart along the length of the batten.

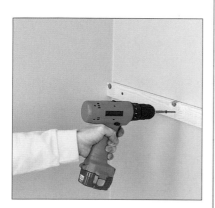

using wall plugs

Wall plugs can be used for making fixings in both solid and hollow walls. A different type of plug is required for each type of wall surface and you will need to check the packet. In this example a solid wall is again shown.

1 Drill into the wall through the batten. In some cases an electric power drill may be a more suitable choice than a cordless drill/ driver, especially if the wall is made from particularly strong material.

2 Press a wall plug into the hole and then insert a screw into the plug. Use a hammer to gently tap the screw and plug further into the wall, until the screw will go no further without a considerable increase in the force applied with the hammer. You will need to tighten up the screw after hammering it in to make absolutely sure the fixture is solid. Employ a cordless drill/driver for this. Continue to add further wall plug fixtures along the batten as required.

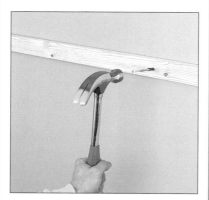

fitting legs

Whether you have purchased a flat-pack or solid carcass kitchen, the manufacturer will almost certainly have left you with the job of attaching legs to each unit.

tools for the job

cordless drill/driver

1 Screw up the legs so that they are in the half-way position along the adjusting thread.

2 Position the legs in the pre-drilled holes on the underside of the unit.

3 Fix them in place with the screws supplied. The units are now ready to be fitted.

getting level

47

positioning base units 〃

Having gained a level guideline, attention may now be turned to the job of positioning and fixing the actual units. A spirit level is again the most important tool here, for although the back edge of the units can be aligned against the batten guideline, the front edge must also be resting at the same level. Thus positioning the units before fixing becomes a methodical process of adjusting leg height to ensure the unit is level across all dimensions.

unit fixings

As a final preparation before the units are positioned, any fixing brackets supplied will need to be attached to the units. There are usually just two types of fixing bracket – those for the worktop and those for the wall.

tools for the job

hammer

cordless drill/driver or screwdriver

worktop fixing brackets

These are small plastic blocks that are knocked into pre-drilled holes in the side of the unit. To form the fixing mechanism between the unit and worktop, a screw is inserted through the bracket into the worktop.

wall fixing brackets

These are L-shaped brackets that are fixed to the back corner of the side panels on a unit. Their L-shape means that once the unit is in position

against the wall, a further screw is inserted through the bracket to hold the unit in place.

NON-ADJUSTABLE UNITS

For units without adjustable legs, small wedges should be used to adjust height accordingly. You can cut your own wedges from 5 x 2.5cm (2 x 1in) batten.

positioning & levelling

The kitchen design featured is of a single run of units along one wall. It is best to begin in the corner of the room if possible, and although kitchen units are not too heavy, you might want to employ a helper to lift the larger units into position.

tools for the job

spirit level

cordless drill/driver

clamp

1 Lift the first unit into place in the corner, addressing the back edge to the batten guideline.

2 Adjust leg height by unscrewing or screwing up the legs as required. This will raise or lower the unit as a whole, thereby bringing it to the correct height for levelling with the batten guideline.

3 Hold a spirit level across the top of the unit to make final adjustments on height. The top of the unit should sit flush with the top edge of the batten. Check the position of the unit by holding the level across all directions on top of the unit, adjusting leg height as required.

4 Move the next unit into position adjusting leg height as required and repeating the levelling procedure. Be sure to hold the level across both units to check they are positioned at the same height.

5 Continue to add further units until the entire run is complete, checking they are all level with each other. Clamp adjacent units together for fixing purposes. If the design of your unit does not include pre-drilled holes for joining, then make your own by drilling through the unit at a point that will be hidden by the hinge plate once it is fitted.

6 Screw all the units together to form a tight fixing. Provided they are all level, this will turn what were single units into a rigid, seamless row.

7 Fix the units to the batten by firmly inserting screws through the wall fixing brackets and into the batten on the wall.

wall fixing alternatives

The method demonstrated above is not the only way of fixing units to a wall and some manufacturers may specify their own particular guidelines. Much of this will be due to the depth of the units. The technique shown will work for most unit types. It is vital, however, to check that the depth of worktop you have will not be too shallow if the units are brought forward from the wall surface using only the batten technique. For kitchen units that are either relatively shallow or particularly deep, you may need to consider applying the following alternative techniques.

shallow units

For shallow units, follow the steps described on pages 46–7 for attaching batten guidelines to the wall. In order to account for standard worktop depth, however, the units will have to be set slightly further away from the wall. Use the technique described on the left to gain the correct height of the units. Then attach additional, shorter lengths of batten to provide a solid fixing between the unit and the wall.

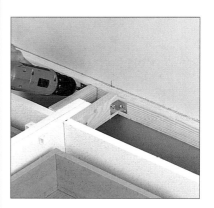

deep units

For deep units it is very likely that the depth of the worktop will be only slightly larger than the actual depth of the unit. As a result, it is essential that the units themselves are positioned as closely as possible to the wall. In this scenario, simply refrain from using a wooden batten to act as a guideline, and instead attach the units directly to the wall, still using wall fixing brackets but carefully following a pencil guideline.

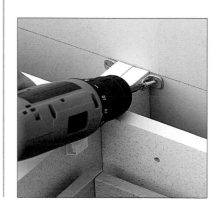

beginning with corner units

On pages 48-9, beginning in the corner of a room was demonstrated using a straight run of base units. However, it is often the case that kitchen layout will require the units to extend around an internal corner. In this situation it is still best to begin in the corner of the room, but clearly the unit used will be a corner base unit rather than a standard base unit. The technique for fitting will therefore need to be modified slightly to account for this variation in design.

fitting kitchen units

50

Corner units can be supplied ready-made, but they are more often supplied part-assembled and require further assembly and levelling, as shown here. Some corner units are designed to have a simple shelf storage system. Another storage option, however, is a carousel system that facilitates access once the unit is fitted. Although a carousel system can be more complicated to fit, the space saving possibilities make it very worthwhile.

tools for the job

cordless drill/driver
hammer
cross head screwdriver
spirit level

1 Add an extra leg to the assembled part of the base unit carcass. This leg is generally positioned directly below the pivotal point for the carousel unit, and will provide extra support for both the unit and carousel when loaded. Adjust leg height to a similar level to that of the other four legs on the unit.

2 Before the unit carcasses are transported they will often be fitted with an internal temporary support to maintain their shape and reduce the risk of damage. Once the extra leg has been fitted and the unit is turned up the correct way, this temporary support may be removed. Following the guidelines provided by the manufacturer, use a hammer to knock in shelf connectors along the edge of the carcass. These will correspond to the attachment of the self-assembly part of the unit.

3 Fix the carousel brake ring into the pre-drilled section at the base of the carcass. Ensure the ring is the correct way around.

4 Thread the top shelf of the carousel onto the supporting pole. Position a supporting dowel or pin through the pole to stop the shelf from slipping down the pole. Then take the second (lower) carousel shelf, and thread it into position. If required, fit a supporting dowel to prevent slipping, as for the first shelf. Attach the lock roller to the underside of the lower shelf, making sure that the arm of the roller is in the correct position as indicated by the manufacturer's guidelines.

tips of the trade

A particularly useful tool to use when you are attempting to align and position kitchen units is a 2m (6ft 6in) spirit level. The length makes it much easier to check the level of a number of units at the same time once they are in position. This is especially useful in L-shaped kitchens where you may wish to allow the level to span from one wall of units across to the other. Although these extended spirit levels are quite expensive, if you are a home improvement enthusiast this tool will prove invaluable for both kitchen installation and future projects.

5 The secured carousel shelves may now be positioned inside the corner unit carcass. Thread the pole up through the top of the carcass before allowing the base of the pole to rest inside the carousel brake ring. Once in position, knock the securing bung in place through the top of the unit. This will hold the pole and carousel securely in place, whilst still allowing it to rotate fully for ease of access.

6 With the carousel securely fitted inside the pre-assembled unit, attention may now be turned to assembling the flat-packed section of the corner unit. Before making a start, however, it is important to take a little time to lay out the pieces in front of you on the floor. This will allow you to identify the different sections as required and make sure each section is around the right way. Once you are familiar with the layout, use a hammer to knock in connectors along the edges of the sections that correspond to the connectors inserted in step 2.

7 Where indicated in the manufacturer's instructions, use corner connecting blocks to join the back section of the unit to what will become the side section of the corner unit as a whole. You will probably find it easier to use a hand-held screwdriver rather than a cordless driver in this situation, since it allows you to maintain greater control while holding the relevant sections in position.

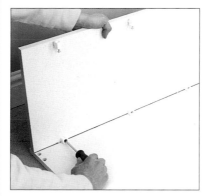

8 Added strength is often given to the join in the floor sections of these units by creating a dowelled join between the floor and side sections. Glue and insert dowels, ensuring that when the floor section is positioned it joins neatly with the side panel. Use a damp cloth to wipe away any excess wood glue before it dries.

9 To complete the self-assembly section of the corner unit, add two further legs to supply support for the unit as a whole once it is assembled. Screw these in place in the usual way.

10 Stand the self-assembled corner section up on its legs and marry up the connectors positioned in steps 2 and 7. Corresponding connectors should simply screw into each other. Again, a hand-held screwdriver is often the best tool for this purpose.

11 Position the finished unit in the corner of the room, adjusting the legs to gain the correct level. Use the spirit level across all angles on top of the unit to ensure precise positioning, as all the other units will take their lead from the position of the corner unit.

fitting wall units ✂✂

As with base units, wall units must also be fitted precisely level to achieve the best possible appearance and in order to function properly, allowing the doors to be opened and closed smoothly. Wall units are reliant on wall fixings to secure them in position, so it is vital that these fixings are correctly installed. Most units are hung on wall brackets and for further strength tend to come already fitted with a fixing rail, where screws can be inserted directly through the back of the unit and into the wall surface. This combination of wall brackets and fixing rail provides the best method for securely positioning wall units.

tools for the job

cordless drill/driver

tape measure

pencil

spirit level

screwdriver

clamp

1 Before taking measurements for wall bracket position, drill some pilot holes in the fixing rail on the back of each of the wall units – two or three holes per unit should be adequate.

2 Measure up from the top of the base units to what will be the bottom edge of the wall units. This distance can vary according to personal preference, but you should bear in mind certain safety issues. Where a wall unit is directly above a hob, the distance must be at least 60cm (2ft). Where units are either side of a hob, a minimum distance of 46cm (1ft 6¼in) is required.

Therefore a good base height for wall units is somewhere between 45–50cm (1ft 6in–1ft 8in). Remember to adjust your measurements to account for the depth of the worktop. The height is measured from the top edge of the worktop, so you will need to add worktop depth on top of unit height.

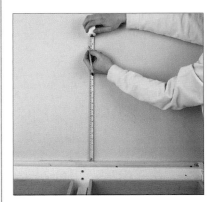

WALL UNIT HEIGHT

To determine the position of wall units you will need to decide what height best suits your needs. A key factor is the stature of the person or persons who most frequently make use of the kitchen facilities – they should not need to overstretch when reaching into cupboards or bang their head when preparing food. Issues of safety should, however, be accounted for. As discussed in step 2, units above and either side of a hob must accord to a minimum height. This minimum often then dictates the height of the other units, as it is better to have an even run of units rather than incorporating a 'step' for the hob.

3 Use the mark made to indicate the height of the units to draw a level pencil guideline. Use a spirit level as a straight edge so that you do not need to make further marks along the wall – simply ensure the bubble remains level. This guideline identifies the base position of all the wall units.

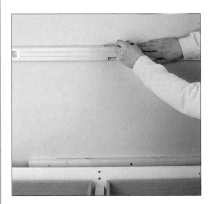

4 Measure up from the base guideline a distance equal to the height of the wall units and draw a further level line to denote what will be their top edge once in place. Paying close attention to the kitchen plan, draw vertical lines to separate the positions of the different wall units.

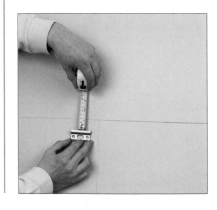

Follow the manufacturer's guidelines to gain the correct distance between the vertical and horizontal guidelines and the edges of each bracket. Mark this position with a pencil.

5 Hold the brackets in place and fix them to the wall with suitable fixings. Remember to choose the correct type of wall plug depending on whether it is a solid or hollow wall. Continue to fit wall brackets for each unit. Most units will require two brackets, one for each corner.

safety advice

When drilling and fixing into walls, take care not to coincide fixings with supply pipes or cables. Use a pipe and cable detector to help avoid such instances.

6 Simply hook the wall unit over the brackets to hold it in position on the wall. For larger units it may be worthwhile employing a helper to lift the unit into place.

7 Once all the units are in place, some minor adjustment may be required for final levelling purposes. In the top internal corner of the units, there is normally an adjustment block that has two functions: one screw can be tightened or loosened to adjust the height of the unit, the other is used to tighten the unit against the wall bracket once you are satisfied that it is totally level. In order to gain access to these screws, it may be necessary to remove a shelf from inside the unit.

8 Wall units should always be mechanically joined together to ensure they create a rigid storage structure. To make a fixing, clamp together adjacent units and drill directly through the side panel of one unit into the next. Position the hole close to the front edge, in line with the hinge fixings.

9 Use two-part steel connection screws to join the units together, inserting two fixings along each unit edge. Tighten with a screwdriver.

10 As an extra precaution to ensure the unit structure is solid, fix directly through the back of the unit by inserting screws through the holes drilled in step 1.

tips of the trade

The methods recommended in order to achieve a strong fixing with screws inserted in the fixing rail, will vary according to the type of screw and wall surface.

• If the wall has to be plugged, you will need to pre-drill holes in the wall surface, so that the screw may be inserted once the wall unit is in place. To make this plugged fixing, after step 7 mark through the drilled hole in the fixing rail, remove the wall unit and then drill and plug the wall before repositioning the unit.

• On solid walls, use concrete anchor screws so that plugging is not necessary.

• Where the drilled hole in the fixing rail coincides with wooden studs in a hollow wall, there is no need for plugging as a standard screw will fix directly into the stud.

fitting doors & drawer fronts

Doors, drawer fronts and handles add the finishing touch to a kitchen unit. Although the fixing procedure for all these items is very straightforward, because they contribute so much to the finished look of a kitchen it is important to take the time to ensure correct technique is employed.

tools for the job

cordless drill/driver

screwdriver

cupboard doors

Most manufacturers pre-cut holes on the inside of doors to indicate the exact hinge position, and pre-drill holes on the unit for the hinge plate. Nevertheless, precision is still vital when inserting screws to ensure the door functions smoothly.

1 Position hinges on the inside of the door and screw them in place securely.

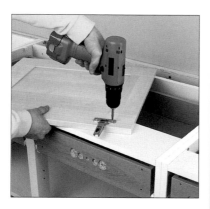

tips of the trade

Always select the correct size of screw for each item. If the screws are too long they will penetrate through to the front of the drawer or door front.

2 Fix hinge plates in the pre-drilled holes in the carcass. A cordless drill/driver is the ideal tool to use so that the screws bite firmly, but set it on a low speed to maintain good control with the driver.

3 Position the door so the hinges slip over the hinge plates, then tighten the retaining screws.

4 If the door height needs to be adjusted to level up the edges,

this can be done by loosening off the hinge plate screws allowing the door to be moved up or down.

5 Tightening or undoing the hinge screw allows further adjustment of door position to gain a level when the door is closed. One screw may require tightening while the other screw needs loosening.

fitting handles

Manufacturers generally make a small indentation on the inside of doors as a guide for fixing handles.

1 Using the correct-sized drill bit – it should match the shank of the handle screw – drill through the

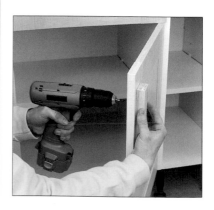

door from the inside out to the front. Hold a block of wood against the door front at the point where the drill bit will break through. This will prevent the surface of the door splintering. You may need to drill more than one hole depending upon your chosen handle design.

2 Insert the handle retaining screw(s) through the hole(s) just drilled.

3 Secure the handle in place by tightening the screw(s).

corner unit doors

The door fronts of corner units tend to require slightly different fitting techniques, due to the variety of designs that facilitate access to the awkward storage space. Technique will also vary according to whether the doors are 'full height', in that they make up the total height of the unit, or whether dummy drawer fronts need to be attached prior to fitting.

full height option

With corner units, a post is attached to the inside edge of one of the doors for a seamless appearance when the doors are closed. Secure the post in place by attaching fixing plates to the back of the door that overlap onto the corner post. Follow the same procedures described above for fixing doors and handles to the corner unit.

170°-opening option

Alternative hinges are available for corner units that are slightly more complex in design in that they can be opened to 170°, making access to inside the unit much easier.

dummy drawer option

In this situation, further fixing plates are used to overlap between the door and drawer front. Thus when the unit is in a closed position it appears to function like separate cupboards and drawers, where in fact the corner unit is only a cupboard.

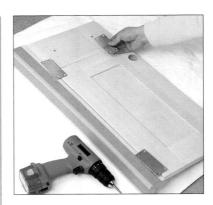

fitting drawer fronts

Check the manufacturer's guidelines as to whether handles need to be attached before the drawer fronts are screwed in, or afterwards.

1 Marry up the pre-drilled holes and double check the drawer front is the right way around.

2 Screw through the pre-drilled holes inside the drawer into the drawer front to secure it in place. Hold the front in position to ensure a good tight fixing.

fitting wooden worktop

Most varieties of worktop are fitted using similar techniques common to all types, although techniques can vary in particular cases. For example, wooden worktop is not always supplied with a moulded edge, so if you wish to create one this will come down to individual choice. You may also need to take into account variations in cutting techniques and plan so that the best use is made of the factory edges on the worktop material.

deciding on cut positions

Factory cut edges on a worktop will be much more accurate than those cut at home, so the best use should be made of them. The diagram opposite shows the ideal arrangement of cut edges for a typical worktop formation. The ends you cut yourself should form junctions with the walls, so that their edges will be covered by final finishing on the walls. In this design, only one cut end is exposed as a visible edge, and with further finishing the cut will in effect be hidden. It is best to join the sides to factory cut ends in order to achieve a precise fit.

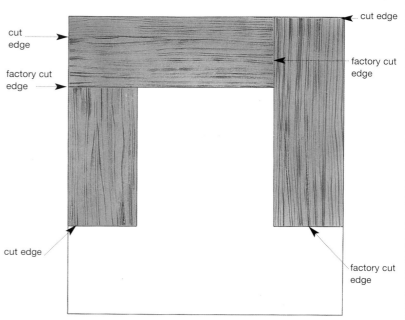

cut edge

cut edge

factory cut edge

factory cut edge

cut edge

factory cut edge

tools for the job

panel saw or jigsaw

tape measure & pencil

clamp

router

fitting a straight run

A straight worktop run is the easiest to fit, but the same techniques can be used for more complex designs.

1 Cut the worktop to length and position it approximately on top of the units. Measure the overhang at the front. If the units have been fitted correctly, this distance should

be slightly more than the required overhang. Normal overhangs are between 0.5 and 2cm ($\frac{1}{8}$ and $\frac{3}{4}$in), measuring from the door or drawer front. Undulations in the shape of the wall may cause the initial overhang to vary slightly along the length of the worktop. Rather than simply trimming a specific length off the back of the

worktop, therefore, you may need to cut away a more graduated portion. To do this, first position the worktop so that its front edge overhangs by the same amount along the entire run of units, while ensuring that the back edge is touching the wall in at least one place.

tips of the trade

Cutting to length – Wooden worktop can be cut with a jigsaw or panel saw. Make sure the correct blade has been fitted if you are using a jigsaw as anything too coarse will splinter the edges of the cut. If using a panel saw, keep the angle of the blade shallow in relation to the worktop surface to produce the cleanest possible cut.

The next step is to make a scribing block to help work out how much of the back edge requires cutting away. The size of the scribing block will be equal to the distance between the front edge of the work surface and the carcass, less whatever distance you wish for the finished overhang of the worktop. Cut a small block of wood to this exact size. Hold a pencil next to the block and draw a guideline by sliding the block along the back wall. You may wish to clamp the work surface in position to ensure it does not move during this procedure.

Cut along the guideline using a jigsaw or panel saw. Accuracy is important, but any small splinters caused by the jigsaw can be sanded away and will, in any case, be hidden when the worktop is fitted against the wall surface.

Reposition the worktop so that the cut back edge is tight against the wall, with the front edge forming an even overhang along the front of the unit. Clamp the worktop in position, screwing through the brackets if supplied. Also fix up into the underside of the worktop through the front fixing rail of the units.

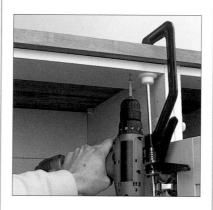

dealing with corners

Corners should not present too many problems, provided that the ideal positioning for cut edges has been taken into account – follow the layout indicated by the diagram opposite. Separate lengths should be cut to size and scribed as required, before joining together.

At the corner join, apply a generous amount of wood glue or pva along the joint.

Move the sections into position, creating a strong bond. Wipe away excess glue with a cloth before it dries. Some manufacturers supply fixing plates that can be attached on the underside of the joint to help hold it firmly in position.

finishing the edge

A router is the ideal tool to add a decorative edge to the worktop. Choose the cutter according to the type of finished edge you require.

Follow the manufacturer's guidelines for the router and lock the cutter in position.

Run the router along the edge of the worktop to create a moulded edge. Work in smooth, continuous motions – by dwelling in particular areas you can singe the wood.

fitting other worktop

Aside from the many wooden varieties, there are a number of other types of worktop available in a range of materials (see pages 28–9 for a fuller discussion of worktop types). Fitting natural and synthetic stone worktops should really be left to the professionals, but laminate worktop can be fitted using a similar technique to wooden worktop, with only slight changes in terms of planning and procedure.

deciding on cut positions

The arrangement of cut edges for laminate worktops is similar to that indicated for wooden worktops on page 56. It equally follows that cut ends should, if possible, be positioned against wall junctions so that their edge will be covered by whatever finish is applied to the wall. However, since laminate worktops cannot be sanded and their edges are not finished by routing, it is even more important to position factory cut edges at the exposed ends. Joining strips can be used to neaten the effect of inaccurate cuts in corners.

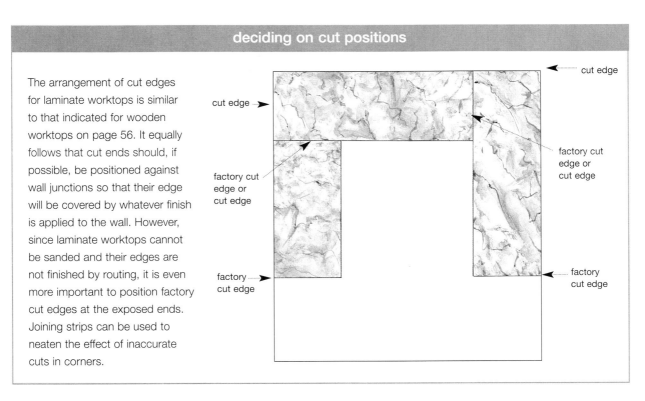

cut edge

cut edge

factory cut edge or cut edge

factory cut edge or cut edge

factory cut edge

factory cut edge

tools for the job

tape measure & pencil

straight edge (batten)

panel saw or jigsaw

hacksaw

cordless drill/driver

cutting worktop

Laminate worktops may be cut with either a panel saw or jigsaw. If using a jigsaw it is vital to choose a blade designed for cutting through laminates, otherwise the surface of the worktop can splinter. Cutting the worktop with the underside uppermost further reduces the risk of splintering.

1 Mark off the required length and draw a precise guideline across the width of the worktop using a length of batten as a straight edge.

2 Move the batten to one side of the guideline, a distance equal to that between the edge of the jigsaw and its blade. Screw the

batten in place, securely but temporarily, at this point on the underside of the worktop. Cut through the worktop holding the jigsaw against the batten. This method produces a perfectly straight cut. Ensure the worktop is well supported when cutting, as any shift in position will risk splitting the laminate surface.

dealing with corners

It is extremely difficult to make an accurate cut across the laminate worktop so that it can be glued and fixed in the same way as for wooden worktop. Even the slightest blemish in a cut or unevenness in positioning will magnify any problems with the join. To overcome this problem, joining strips are commonly used to create a strong join between sections.

1 Cut the joining strip to the exact width required for the laminate worktop – strips are usually made from aluminium, which can be cut using a hacksaw.

2 Apply some silicone sealant along the cut edge of the worktop, and then screw the joining strip in place along the edge.

3 Add a further quantity of silicone sealant along the facing edge of the adjoining worktop section, which should already be fitted in place on the unit. Then slide the section with the joining strip into position flush against the edge covered with sealant.

4 Screw through the fixing rails in the carcass into the underside of the worktop. Pay special attention at the corner. Wipe away any excess then allow the silicone to dry and create a watertight bond.

tips of the trade

Fitting straight lengths – To fit straight lengths of laminate worktop follow the same technique described for wooden worktop on pages 56–7. Simply check the correct jigsaw blade is installed for cutting laminate finish.

finishing edges

The manufacturer will have provided laminate strips to finish the worktop ends. These are applied using a warm iron, which melts and activates an adhesive on the back of the laminate strip sticking it securely in place.

tools for the job

iron
scissors
craft knife

1 Heat the iron to the temperature specified by the manufacturer. Cut the laminate strip to size with scissors and hold it against the worktop edge. Gently run the iron across the surface of the strip until it bonds. Once the adhesive has dried and the strip is securely positioned, trim the edge of the strip to ensure a neat and precise finish – a craft knife is ideal for this purpose.

WORKTOP OPTIONS

• **Natural stone –** To fit a natural stone worktop, such as granite, create a template of the area required first and give this to the factory for them to cut it to the correct size and polish. The worktop is fitted in large sections, which is best carried out by professional fitters. An epoxy-based resin is normally used for dealing with joints. Since the stone has no elasticity, it is vital that the units are exactly level – any undulations will cause the stone to crack under its own weight.

• **Synthetic stone –** This type of worktop also needs to be templated for fitting, which is best undertaken by professionals. A level surface is similarly crucial for fitting.

fitting cornice, pelmet & end panels ⚡⚡

Cornice, pelmet and end panels provide finishing touches to units and are used as decorative embellishments to improve the overall appearance of the kitchen. These items have no structural role to play and are primarily concerned with hiding fixings and 'rounding off' the edges and sides of units, to create a pleasing finished appearance.

tools for the job

tape measure & pencil
mitresaw
cordless drill/driver
sealant gun
clamp

fitting cornice

Cornice is the decorative edging fitted around the top edge of wall units to provide a moulded and framed finish to the run, enhancing the 'built-in' look. Fixings are hidden from view when inserted through the cornice top down into the unit tops. Fitting cornice is a process of careful measuring and fixing, and accuracy is especially important for fitting cornice round a corner.

1 Observe how the design of the cornice will relate to the fitting process, then measure the required length and cut the two pieces to size. Mark on the end of each piece the

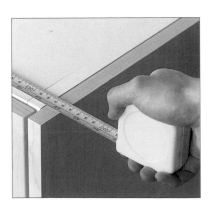

45°-angle cut required to form the mitre joint. You will usually need to align the cornice with the 90°-angle made by the corner of the wall unit carcass. However, if the unit includes an end panel and/or door extending out slightly from the carcass, you will need to take this into account.

2 Make the angled cut on the cornice using a mitresaw for accuracy. Ensure the saw is well supported to prevent tearing the cornice surface as the cut is made.

3 Screw the first section of cornice in position allowing the screws to bite firmly into the wall unit. Be sure

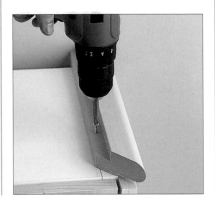

to use screws of the appropriate length so that they do not penetrate through to inside the unit.

4 Apply some wood glue or pva to the end of the fixed section before attaching the next piece.

5 Position the next cornice piece, forming the mitre joint by hand initially, allowing the glue to produce a tight bond. Continue by screwing the cornice in place employing the same technique described in step 3.

6 In some cases a tiny gap may appear in the mitre joint. Fill the gap with silicone sealant of a similar

colour to the cornice. Wipe away excess with a cloth before it dries.

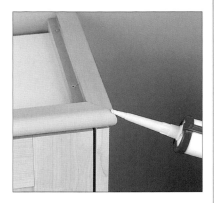

fitting pelmet

Many manufacturers produce one shape of moulding that can act for both cornice and pelmet, such is their similarity. The main difference is that pelmet is attached to the bottom rather than top edge of the unit. As you would expect, the technique for fitting is very similar. Measure and cut the pelmet as for cornice, however you will need to clamp the pelmet in place to allow it to be fixed to the underside of the units.

fitting end panels

End panels are an optional fitting applied to the ends of both wall and base units. They are generally chosen to match the door and drawer fronts.

1 Cut the panel to height, then position it at the end of the unit, overlapping the front edge. Pull the drawer out to allow access for a tape measure and measure the distance required for the panel to overhang the front of the unit. Cut away any extra from the back edge. Most walls are not totally 'square', so it is best to scribe the back edge of the panel to create a neat fit. While measuring the overhang at the front, therefore, allow the panel to touch the wall in at least one place. Then measure and

cut a scribing block, which will produce the required overhang.

2 Draw a guideline along the back edge of the panel using the scribing block to maintain distance.

3 Cut away the unwanted section of panel with a jigsaw using a blade suitable for laminates. Position and clamp the panel at the end of the unit, then insert screws from inside the unit into the back of the panel. Screwing from the inside ensures no damage is visible.

👍
tips of the trade

As an alternative method, apply bonding adhesive or silicone sealant to the end panel before screwing it in place. Thus you will only need one or two screw fixings while the adhesive or sealant dries.

End panels, cornice and pelmet help to lift the appearance of what are essentially functional units in a kitchen design.

fitting plinth 〃

As cornice and pelmet provide a finished edge to wall units, so plinth provides the finished edge to the bottom of base units. For units with legs, plinth is fitted by means of clips attached to the back of the piece of plinth that enable it to be clipped in place on the legs.

tools for the job

tape measure & pencil
mitresaw
panel saw or jigsaw
combination square
cordless drill/driver
iron
scissors
craft knife

1 Plinth is generally supplied in standard lengths of a set height. In most cases, the height will not need to be cut down as units tend to be manufactured so that the plinth fits comfortably underneath. A slight gap in-between the top of the plinth and the underside of the unit should not cause a problem, since this area is not in general view. Before cutting plinth to the correct length, check to see whether you will also need to reduce the height at the same time. Remember this gap may not be consistent under all units, especially if the floor has a slope. You should therefore check the height measurement in several positions.

2 Cut the plinth to the correct length and, if necessary, reduce in height. You can use a panel saw or jigsaw to cut the plinth across its width, but a mitresaw, set to a 90°-angle, will provide a cleaner and more accurate cut, ensuring the best possible joins with other sections. Use a panel saw or jigsaw to adjust the plinth height.

3 Lay out the cut length of plinth in front of the base units allowing its bottom edge to rest against the unit legs (the front of the plinth should be facing down). Use a combination square and pencil to draw a series of lines on the back of the plinth to correspond with the centre of each base leg.

4 Fix clip brackets in the centre of each guideline. Make sure the screws being used are not too long. Otherwise they will penetrate through to the front face of the plinth and cause unsightly damage.

5 Position the clips in each of the brackets so they are still aligned with the base unit legs.

6 If a sealant strip is supplied, turn the plinth upside down and attach the strip to the bottom edge. The purpose of a sealant strip is to create a neat, watertight seal that facilitates cleaning.

7 Having applied the sealant strip – if applicable, otherwise after the clips have been positioned – turn the plinth back up the right way and clip it in position on the base unit legs.

8 Once again check the plinth height. If flooring is yet to be laid, bear in mind it is best for the flooring material to extend under the units, with the plinth fitting neatly on top. Use a piece of card or board similar in height to your choice of flooring to check for adequate tolerance. If you find there is not enough, unclip the plinth and cut down the height further.

internal corners

Internal corners present a slight problem when dealing with plinths, as it is unlikely that a leg will fall precisely on the point where the plinth requires joining. You will therefore need to use another type of bracket, which joins the two plinths together to form a rigid enough connection so that both ends are held securely in place.

1 Cut the two lengths of plinth so that one length extends slightly further under the units than would be the case for an exact corner join. Lay this longer length on the floor so that the front is facing upwards. Secure a fixing bracket on the front face in a central position slightly back from the point where the two sections of plinth will ultimately join.

2 Fix the connecting clip for the corner bracket at the end of the shorter length of plinth on the back face. When the two lengths are positioned, the clip on the back edge of the shorter length will join with the fixing bracket on the longer length, clipping together to form a tight internal joint in the corner.

dealing with cut ends

In some cases the cut end of a length of plinth may be visible, for example, on external corners where there is often no option but to have an exposed end. If this situation arises, employ a similar technique for dealing

with the cut ends of a worktop and cover over the end with a thin strip of laminate (see also page 59).

1 Measure and cut the laminate strips to size with scissors.

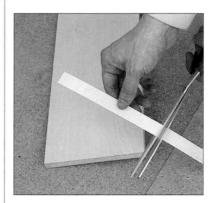

2 Position the strip on the end of the plinth, then smooth over the strip with a warm iron – the heat from the iron causes the adhesive to bond with the cut end. As it is a contact adhesive there is no need for clamping. Once it is secure, trim the strip with a craft knife for a neat finish.

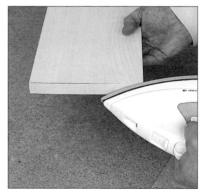

> **PLINTH OPTIONS**
>
> Although fitted kitchens normally include specially manufactured plinth, it is possible to make your own using either mdf or prepared softwood planks. The same procedure is used for fixing the plinth in place, but the main benefit with this method is that more options for finishing are available. For example, planking can be stained to provide a natural look.

fitting breakfast bars ⁊⁊⁊

Breakfast bars are becoming an increasingly popular addition to kitchen design. They can be built separate and free-standing or integrated into a run of fitted units, thus transforming a worktop into a multi-purpose area that can be used for both food preparation and eating. What fundamentally changes a worktop into a breakfast bar is the ability to sit comfortably at the worktop so that meals may be taken.

separate bars

Separate breakfast bars are ideal for individuals or couples and are a good way of using worktop offcuts.

tools for the job

tape measure & pencil
panel saw or jigsaw
cordless drill/driver
spirit level
hacksaw

1 Cut 5 x 2.5cm (2 x 1in) batten to a length equal to what will be the back edge of the breakfast bar. Chamfer the ends of the batten so that they will not be visible when the worktop is in position. Screw the batten to the wall at a suitable height. This need not be standard worktop height – the ability to sit comfortably should be the deciding factor.

2 Attach L-shaped fixing brackets along the batten at roughly 20cm (8in) intervals. Make sure that the top section of the brackets extends horizontally and flush with the top edge of the batten.

3 Cut a section of worktop to size. Adding a curved edge to the corners will help soften its appearance. To form the curved edge, make a guideline – you can use the base of a paint can for a template – then cut along the guideline with a jigsaw.

4 Hold the worktop in position, sitting on the batten, and rest a spirit level on the surface. Make any adjustments needed to get the worktop level, then measure the distance from the underside of the worktop to the floor.

5 Using a hacksaw, cut a length of stainless steel tubing to this measurement. With suitable brackets, attach the pole to the underside of the worktop and floor. Fix the worktop securely in place through the L-shaped fixing brackets along the back edge. The edge of the worktop may now be routed for final finishing (see page 57).

integrated bars

An integrated breakfast bar is basically a continuation of the kitchen worktop, with the option to be much deeper or wider than standard size. As such, much of the fitting procedure is similar to that demonstrated on pages 56–9.

tools for the job

tape measure & pencil
hand saw or jigsaw
cordless drill/driver
spirit level
hammer

1 It is always best to fit a breakfast bar before the rest of the kitchen worktop, because of its greater size, even though it may not be fixed as the first section. Breakfast bars are often supplied in a specific size, although wooden ones may be cut down and the edge finished yourself. Measure the worktop to work out the different overhangs. As with a normal worktop, the non-seating edge should have an overhang of between 0.5cm (¹⁄₈in) and 2cm (³⁄₄in). The opposite overhang should be deep enough for people to be seated comfortably.

2 On the seating side of the bar, it will be necessary to provide some sort of finish to the back of the

kitchen units. Tongue and groove panelling offers an attractive and hardwearing option. You will need to build a framework to attach the panelling – 5 x 2.5cm (2 x 1in) or 5 x 5cm (2 x 2in) batten is ideal for this purpose. Gain a secure fixing by the wall and continue to build up the framework.

3 Horizontal struts will need to be included in the batten framework to provide additional strength and extra fixing points for the tongue and groove panelling.

4 Once the framework is complete simply build up the panels by fixing through the tongues of each board into the batten struts below. Join each new length over the previous panel to hide the fixing points.

tips of the trade

Breakfast bars with a considerable overhang may need to be fitted with extra support. This can be provided by screwing a length of batten at the wall junction underneath the overhang.

Here a run of floor units has been fitted with a worktop that overhangs on one side so that it may be used for both dining and food preparation.

boxing in

One of the attractive features of a fitted kitchen is that most of the exposed cables and pipes are hidden by the units themselves. Sometimes, however, a small amount of boxing in may be required to cover unsightly features still exposed after the units have been fitted. There are two main types of boxing – that which covers over permanently and that which incorporates a built-in access hatch of some variety.

without access

Boxing in without access is by far the easiest to build of the two types, as it is simply a case of making the most unobtrusive boxing design possible. The most versatile materials for building any type of boxing are mdf in conjunction with 5 x 2.5cm (2 x 1in) batten.

tools for the job

tape measure & pencil

panel saw or jigsaw

cordless drill/driver

hammer

1 Pipes are one of the most common obstacles to be dealt with by boxing and are often found in the corners of rooms. First of all, fix cut lengths of batten to the wall surface on either side of the pipes.

2 Measure the dimensions required to make a box with two pieces of mdf. Remember that one piece will have to overlap the other in order to create a right-angled join.

3 Cut the mdf to size using a jigsaw or panel saw. If using a panel saw, remember to keep the angle of the blade shallow in relation to the surface of the mdf – this will improve both the ease of cutting and the accuracy of the cut.

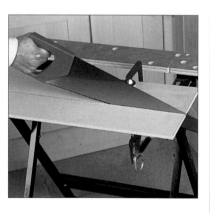

safety advice

Mdf creates more dust when sawn than other fibreboards, so whether cutting with a jigsaw or panel saw, always wear a dust mask.

4 Nail the mdf sheets in place with panel pins. Start off the pins by knocking them along the edge of the mdf before it is in position. This makes the final nailing much easier and reduces the chance of damaging the wall with the hammer.

5 Nail the second piece in place, then add further pins along the edge of the overlapping sheet to form a strong corner joint. The boxing can now be painted or tiled as required.

tips of the trade

Cracks along the junction made by the boxing can be filled with flexible caulk before decorating. Flexible filler reduces the risk of cracking, especially important when boxing over hot water pipes where temperature changes cause the boxing to expand and contract slightly.

with access

Access is generally required when a stopcock or stop valve is present in a section of pipework. Whatever the situation, access panels can be hinged, fitted with magnetic catches or can even be built as free-standing units that are positioned without any permanent fixing. Free-standing units are a common type of boxing for below boilers in kitchens, where access is required – a small free-standing boxing unit is placed over the pipework to shield it from view.

tools for the job

tape measure & pencil

panel saw

cordless drill/driver

jigsaw

screwdriver

hacksaw

hammer

hinged access

1 Having cut an mdf panel to fit your boxing framework, mark off the size of door required in the face of the mdf. A tile makes an excellent template and is an ideal size for a hatch that needs to be large enough for hand access.

2 Using a flathead drill bit, drill through the mdf at each corner of what will be the access panel

opening. Be careful not to allow the edge of the drill bit to extend over the pencil guidelines.

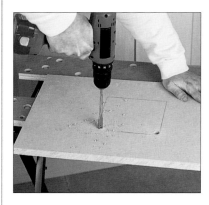

3 The drilled holes will act as an access point so for a jigsaw to cut out the panel.

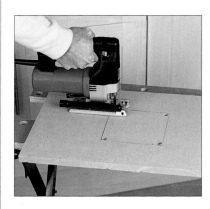

4 Cut a door to fit in the hole in the panel from another piece of mdf. Then use a hacksaw to cut a length of piano hinge and screw it into the hinging edge of the panel door.

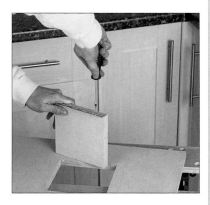

5 Fit a small handle to the door before finally screwing it in place on the hinging edge of the panel.

The entire panel may now be attached to the boxing framework following the same method described opposite.

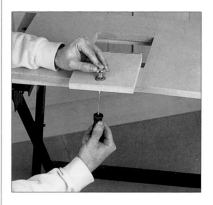

free-standing access

1 Cut pieces of mdf to size and fix them together along one edge to create a right-angled unit.

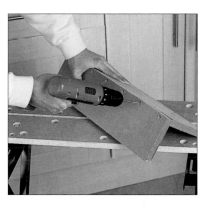

2 On the inside of the unit, glue additional blocks to the right-angled junction, thereby enhancing the structural strength. The unit can now be tiled over or painted and positioned on a worktop, covering pipework that needs periodic access.

fitting kitchen accessories

Kitchen accessories are usually fitted after the units and worktop have been installed. The reason for this is that most accessories require fitting into unit carcasses or cutting into worktop, and it is essential that units are permanently positioned before this process takes place. Most of the work can easily be carried out by a competent home improvement enthusiast. It is only with the final connection of appliances that you may require the services of a professional tradesperson to deal with gas, plumbing or electrics. This chapter looks at the main accessories and appliances found in kitchen designs and demonstrates the best techniques for installation.

Hood-style extractor fans are becoming increasingly popular kitchen accessories, for their looks and practical application.

accessory options

Kitchen accessories and appliances are often the most expensive items purchased when fitting a new kitchen, which makes it all the more important that correct fitting procedures and techniques are followed. As with most kitchen items, a wide variety of options is available allowing for ever greater freedom of expression to determine both the style and practical functioning of your kitchen. Different styles of accessories usually require different methods for fitting in place, and the manufacturer's guidelines should be adhered to at all times.

contemporary sink units

Contemporary trends have made integral sink units a popular choice for kitchens. The standard unit comprises a sink, drainer and central bowl, positioned in a cut hole in the worktop to create an integrated effect. Larger options are also available, including units with one and a half or two sinks. Modern sink units are most often made from stainless steel with no additional colouring, and this type of finish has proved popular for its sleek and hygienic appearance. Units are also available in numerous colours, and before buying you need to consider carefully what type of sink will best fit in with the decor of the kitchen and appearance of the other units.

RIGHT *Such is the unobtrusiveness of integral sink units that they practically 'disappear' into unit and worktop structure. Often only the tap fittings stand out, so the addition of attractive taps offers scope for enhancing the overall appearance.*

traditional sink units

A Belfast sink is the ideal accessory if you are trying to achieve a traditional look for your kitchen. As well as helping to create a nostalgic feel, they are also highly functional accessories that can deal with all manner of washing requirements. A practical issue to consider, however, is that due to their excessive weight, Belfast sinks will normally need to be supported on brick piers built up from floor level. In this regard it will be essential to ensure that the piers are constructed to exactly the same height so that the sink will be positioned level.

LEFT *The traditional look is further enhanced by cutting a Belfast sink into a wooden worktop. It is essential to have the top edge of the sink corresponding exactly with the bottom edge of the worktop so that a good watertight seal may be achieved.*

integral cooker and hood

The popularity of the built-in look has grown to the stage where nearly all accessories or appliances can be made to fit seamlessly within the kitchen design. Extractor fans above cookers can be built to appear entirely in keeping with the run of wall units, and likewise the front face of the cooker itself. Indeed, the hob is often the only visible clue to where the cooker is positioned in a kitchen.

RIGHT *In this example, false drawer fronts and cupboard fronts have been fitted below the hob to minimize disruption to the overall appearance of the bank of fitted units, while the extractor fan has been housed within a decorative unit that again matches the rest of the kitchen.*

separate cooker and hood

The obvious alternative to the integrated look of cooker and hood is to produce a distinctive set-up whereby the cooker and extractor fan form separate units, but are still fitted into the overall kitchen design. In such cases, the extractor fan takes the form of a hood and chimney that can provide extra lighting as well as removing fumes from the kitchen.

RIGHT *Although the cooker and hood constitute separate units, this design can still appear to be part of the fitted kitchen look. Indeed, manufacturers have developed this type of cooker set-up into an attractive feature that can act as a focal point to the kitchen – where, after all, cooking is the essential activity.*

integral washing appliances

Dishwashers and washing machines are not the most attractive of kitchen accessories, and it is therefore often a good idea to integrate such items into a run of kitchen units. Manufacturers produce many different designs for door and drawer frontage systems that can be used to hide these appliances. The practice of integrating appliances can also be extended to fridges and freezers.

LEFT *The dishwasher in this kitchen has been 'hidden' in the left-hand bank of units, with a false door fitted over the front so that only the black dial panel is visible. 'Hiding' a dishwasher helps to maintain a continuous line and finish and makes the best use of available space due to the precise fit.*

fitting sink units

The first stage of the procedure for fitting a sink unit is to measure and cut a hole for the sink in the worktop. Attention is then turned to the different elements of the sink itself, with the taps needing to be attached and waste system installed. Finally, connect the unit to water and waste pipes.

safety advice

If you have a metal sink, and/or any metal pipes, they must be earth bonded for safety reasons. Contact a qualified electrician to carry this out.

tools for the job

tape measure & pencil

cordless drill/driver

jigsaw

paintbrush

screwdriver

adjustable spanners

1 Often a paper template will be provided as a guide for cutting. If not, turn the sink upside down on the worktop, then measure to ensure it is fitted equidistant from the front and back edges of the worktop. Make sure the sink is correctly positioned in relation to the base unit below.

2 Draw a pencil guideline around the edge of the sink, making sure it does not slip as you do so.

3 Take a further measurement of the overlap where the sink edge will rest on the worktop once fitted. Mark this guideline inside the first.

4 Use a slot-head drill bit to drill holes through the worktop in

the corners of this second pencil guideline – these holes will allow access for a jigsaw blade. Be careful not to allow the drill bit to break the bounds of this guideline.

5 Cut around the inside guideline to remove the internal area of worktop. When you approach the finishing cut, ensure the worktop is well supported so that you do not risk damaging or splitting it.

6 If the sink is being fitted in a wooden worktop, as shown here, apply a coat of oil around the cut edge to seal it from the possibility of water penetration once the sink is in use. Attention may now be turned to the sink unit itself.

7 Insert your chosen taps into the sink unit. Make sure that the backnut and required washers are fitted to the underside of the tap and that supply pipes are attached. Although tap designs do vary and you should take account of the manufacturer's specific guidelines.

8 Now attach the waste system to the sink, again following the manufacturer's guidelines.

9 Fix retaining clips around the raised strip on the underside lip of the sink unit.

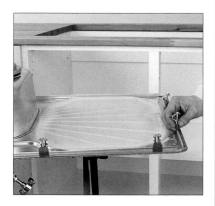

👍

tips of the trade

You will find It is much easier to carry out the procedures for inserting taps and attaching the waste system and retaining clips (steps 7–9) before the sink is fitted in place, as access to the unit is clearly much easier.

10 Turn the sink the correct way up and lower it into the cut hole in the work surface. It should be a tight but comfortable fit.

11 Screw up the retaining clips on the underside of the sink – these should bind with the worktop to form a watertight seal. The sink and taps may now be connected to the waste and water supply, respectively. If the sink is similarly positioned to the old one then this is quite a simple procedure as the pipes will be in close proximity. For instructions on how to connect and, if necessary, re-route these services, see pages 42–3. If in any doubt seek professional advice.

REVERSIBLE UNITS

Some units include a reversible feature, whereby a tap hole is cut on both sides so that the sink can be positioned with the drainer on either side. If you have such a unit then you will need to fit a bung in the front of the sink before final connection.

This fitted sink unit features false drawer fronts to maintain the illusion of a continuous bank of storage units. Dummy drawer fronts are fixed with special brackets.

fitting an integral hob & oven

If you are looking to create a compact and neat overall appearance to your kitchen, then fitting an integral hob and oven will help considerably to realize this aim. The integrated effect is achieved by the fact that the oven and hob are housed, or appear to be housed, within the general make-up of a run of units. Some manufacturers produce specific units to hold these appliances or, in the case of ovens especially, brackets are used to suspend the appliance between two units. Whatever design you choose, the correct electrical and/or gas supply will need to be connected. Professional help will almost certainly be required for this purpose (see also pages 42-3).

hobs

Cutting the worktop to accommodate a hob requires a very similar technique to that used for fitting sink units. The same basic method for measuring guidelines and cutting out the worktop can be applied to hobs. Refer to pages 72–3, adapting as required.

tools for the job

tape measure & pencil
cordless drill/driver
jigsaw
screwdriver

1 It is usually the case that the manufacturers will stipulate a minimum distance between the back wall and the edge of the hob. This minimum is required for obvious safety reasons and practicalities – adequate space must be left in order to connect up electrics and/or gas pipes, and for cooking the hob needs to be positioned far enough away from the wall so that pans can sit comfortably on the back rings.

2 Once the hole has been cut, lower the hob in place and use clips to secure it in the worktop. The hob may then be connected up to the gas or electric supply as required – a job for a professional. Even if the hob is gas powered, as shown in this example, it is likely that an electrical connection will also be required to supply the ignition system.

ovens

Although ovens are often housed in purpose-made units, they may also be suspended using a system of runners, as demonstrated here. With this system, the worktop and all the carcasses of a run of units must first be fitted, leaving the appropriate size of gap between units into which the oven can be fitted. The runner system is a simple and effective way to create an integrated appearance.

tips of the trade

It is best to fit plinth to a run of units after the oven has been installed, so that the height can be adjusted to ensure the oven door opens and closes properly. Your oven design may also include a ventilation grill – follow the manufacturer's guidelines for fitting the grill into the plinth.

tools for the job

cordless drill/driver
tape measure & pencil
screwdriver
spirit level

1 The first step is to fix the two vertical runners (or rails) along the front edge of the units on either side of the gap left in the run for inserting the oven. To ensure accuracy, you may find it useful to form pilot holes with a cordless drill before inserting the screws.

2 Fix both of the vertical rails in place, screwing through the ready-made holes provided along the length of each rail.

3 Mark off the positions for the bottom horizontal runners – this will normally be slightly back from the front edge of the units. Make sure the runners are positioned precisely level and at the height recommended by the manufacturer, according to the type of oven being fitted.

4 Again, drill pilot holes for the fixings and secure the horizontal runners in place.

5 Check that there is enough depth between the front of the worktop and back wall so that the oven will fit comfortably.

6 Attach further runners to the oven itself, along the bottom edge of both side sections – these runners will be supplied along with the oven. Follow the manufacturer's guidelines to ensure that they are fitted using the correct technique and at precisely the right level.

7 Lift and slide the oven in place, allowing the oven runners to rest on the runners attached to the unit.

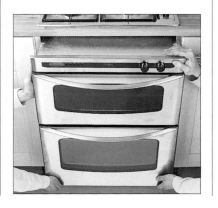

8 The front edge of the oven should overlap onto the vertical runners fixed to the sides of the units. Drill a pilot hole through the marked positions on the oven edge and into the rails. Use a drill bit suitable for cutting through the metal surface of the runners.

9 Finally, insert screws in the pilot holes through the overlap and into the vertical runners, thereby securing the oven in place.

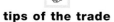

tips of the trade

Supply connection – To allow for access, electrical and gas supplies will need to be connected before the oven is finally installed. Fitting a kitchen is an exact process, however, and prior to connection it is necessary to ensure that the correct tolerance has been built in behind the oven to accommodate gas and electrical supplies. Therefore, it is best to fit the oven first to check for tolerance, then remove the oven temporarily to allow access for connection.

fitting an extractor fan & hood

Installing appliances designed to ensure adequate ventilation is now a crucial aspect of fitting a modern kitchen, largely due to the increased effectiveness of general household insulation. Natural drafts prevalent in houses before such innovations as double glazing were generally sufficient for dispelling the build-up of fumes. Today, however, a mechanical means of ventilation is usually required for adequate air circulation. Early designs in this area were uninspiring, but attractive ventilation systems are now available that greatly contribute to kitchen appearance.

Kitchen ventilation systems are generally available either in an integral design, whereby the appliance is built into a run of units, or based on a hood-and-chimney design as shown in this example. Each of the two basic designs can be used with either a ducting or filter extraction system. A ducting system involves the installation of a physical channel from the hood to the outside of the house. A hole large enough to fit a ventilation shaft through an exterior wall will need to be drilled, and as a consequence this system requires a fair amount of work. The alternative is to use a 'recirculator' system that circulates the air through charcoal filters. These filters are easily fitted in the extractor hood, and no ducting is required. Most hood designs are built to accommodate both options and final adjustments can be made during the fitting procedure.

tools for the job

tape measure & pencil

spirit level

cordless drill/driver

screwdriver

1 The manufacturer will stipulate a precise distance requirement between the worktop and bottom edge of the hood. Measure up and mark off this distance on the wall surface. Make the mark central to the position of the hob. You may require a spirit level for this purpose.

2 Attach the supplied template to the wall with masking tape, and mark through at the fixing points.

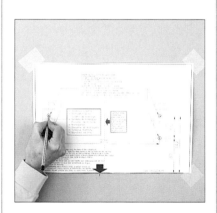

safety advice

It is vital to ensure your kitchen has sufficient ventilation, especially if it includes gas appliances. If you are in any doubt about the adequacy of a particular system, you must seek professional advice.

3 Drill holes into the wall surface at the marked-off points and insert the correct size of wall plug, according to whether the wall is hollow or solid.

4 Screw hood-retaining brackets into the wall ensuring they are precisely vertical and secure.

5 Lift the hood into place and clip it over the wall retaining brackets.

You may need another person to help with the lifting. Check it is positioned centrally in relation to the hob below.

6 Further retaining screws will normally need to be fitted inside the hood to tighten the fixings between the hood and wall bracket. Connect up the electrical supply for the hood at this stage. Professional help will be required for this purpose. If you have chosen a ducted ventilation system, the ducting should also be fitted and connected to the outside vent at this point.

7 Fit the chimney by slotting it into the top of the hood. You will normally also need to attach a bracket to the ceiling. Draw a level vertical guideline from the centre of the hood top to the ceiling, then fix the bracket.

8 Slide the hood into place, and extend the sections to join with the ceiling bracket. Hoods tend to be supplied in two sections so that one slips over the other, making height adjustment a simple procedure.

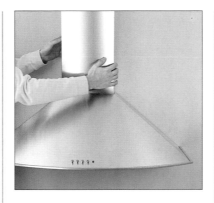

9 Fix through the holes provided at the top of the chimney into the ceiling bracket to secure it in place.

10 With the chimney in place, the only thing remaining is to fit the charcoal filters to the underside of the hood.

safety advice

Charcoal filters need to be replaced periodically to ensure optimum performance. The manufacturer should provide specific information on the working life of a filter and it is important to adhere to their stipulations concerning how often to replace filters.

A large hood-and-chimney extractor fan system offers an impressive feature, and if a light fixture is included this will aid cooking on the hob immeasurably.

fitting a dishwasher & washing machine

Either a washing machine or a dishwasher, or often both, are commonly found in most modern kitchens. Both appliances need to be connected to a water supply and drainage facility and as such are normally situated close to the kitchen sink. Connecting up each appliance involves a similar procedure, with the bulk of the work involved in getting the supply and drainage pipes to the appropriate joints.

plumbing in appliances

Washing machines usually require both a hot and cold water supplies, whereas the majority of dishwashers require only a cold water supply. The most ideal set-up is to have the supply pipe(s) branching off the pipes that supply water to the kitchen sink. These supply pipe(s) are generally situated between the shut-off valves and the taps by means of a 'T'-connector, which directs the supply pipes horizontally away from the main vertical pipes for the sink. A threaded tap connection is needed on the end of these horizontal supply pipes so that the machine supply can be connected easily and the tap turned on to provide water. In order to connect the discharge hose and water supply pipe(s) to the appropriate joint below the sink, access must be made in the back of the kitchen sink unit.

tools for the job

cordless drill/driver

slip-joint pliers

screwdriver

1 Use a hole saw or large flathead drill bit to make holes of the correct diameter for the pipes in the back panel of the unit. In this case a dishwasher is being fitted, which requires two holes to be drilled, one for the cold water supply pipe and the other for the discharge hose.

2 Thread the discharge hose and supply pipe through the holes. For this process the dishwasher needs to be positioned close to the wall, which often makes access tight, though the pipe and hose normally allow enough length.

3 A rubber filter will generally need to be fitted inside the connecting joint for the cold water supply. This filter helps to keep damaging impurities away from the washing mechanism. Once in place, the filter can quite simply be screwed onto the threaded end of the cold water supply pipe.

4 Connect up the discharge hose to a waste adaptor on the sink trap. Ensure the hose leaves the dishwasher vertically, joining the sink trap at a height between 30cm (12in) and 80cm (32in). Never cut down the hose from the supplied length.

fitting integral dishwashers

Integral dishwashers enable separate doors to be attached, so that the dishwasher unit does not detract from the finished look of a fitted kitchen. The plumbing remains the same, but some care will be needed to adjust the washer level and fix the door.

tools for the job

cordless drill/driver

pencil

slip-joint pliers

1 To protect the work surface above the dishwasher from steam and water attack, it is best to fit a condensation strip along the underside. A plastic self-adhesive strip has been used here, but some manufacturers supply a metal strip that requires screwing in place.

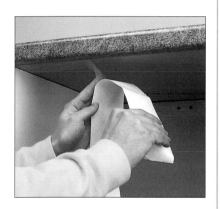

2 If necessary, screw the feet of the dishwasher into the threaded holes on its base. Try to set the feet at approximately the same height. The machine will need to be leant back for this process. Then position the dishwasher in front of its alcove and adjust the feet to gain a perfect level at the correct height. Levelling is vital to ensure the optimum working position and ensure that the door fits correctly and blends with other units.

3 Connect up the water supply and fit the discharge hose using the method already described, then ease the dishwasher into position. You may now turn your attention to fitting the door. Fitted kitchen designs will either provide full doors or, as is shown here, combine the drawer and cupboard front look. In this last case, the false drawer and cupboard fronts need to be connected to each other with metal plate connectors. Simply screw these in place along the joint between the drawer and cupboard fronts, ensuring that edges are kept flush and the joint is tight.

4 Use the template supplied by the manufacturer to mark off the correct positions for the securing brackets on the back of the door.

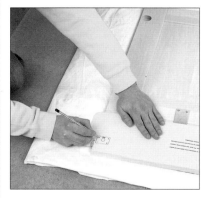

5 Screw the securing brackets in place following the marked-off screw insertion points indicated by the template. Then fit both the drawer and cupboard handles employing the same techniques as demonstrated on pages 54–5.

6 Press the 'door' into position on the front of the dishwasher, marrying up the fixing brackets with the fixing holes on the dishwasher.

7 If appropriate to the door design, fix from the inside through the dishwasher door and into the back of the unit front.

INTEGRAL DOORS

Integral doors may also be fitted to fridges and freezers. Washing machines usually have a separate hinged door, which is attached in a similar way to base units.

flooring

Of all the rooms in a house, it is arguably the kitchen where the floor surface suffers the greatest level of wear and tear. When considering different options of flooring for the kitchen environment, therefore, the most important deciding factors should be the hardwearing properties of a particular material. Each type of floor covering requires a different technique for laying, but whatever the material, an attractive and durable finished floor is achieved as much in the detailed planning of the work as in the actual fitting and finishing process itself. This chapter looks at the main options available and describes the correct techniques for producing the best possible results.

A combination of large and small hard
tiles produces a subtly-patterned and
durable floor surface.

flooring options

The overriding emphasis on producing a hardwearing kitchen floor does not mean there is any marked limitation on the choice available. Flooring as a whole is a growing sector in the home improvement market and kitchens are not excluded from this category. Indeed, many developments in the field of flooring materials have been made with kitchen use specifically in mind. Take for example laminate floors, which until recently would not have been recommended for kitchen use, but are now specifically manufactured for this purpose.

laminate

Varieties of laminate flooring are now manufactured specifically for use in kitchens. As well as providing an attractive finish, laminate floors are also very easy to clean and require little maintenance. When making your choice, however, it is always worth checking to ensure that the particular design is suitable for kitchen use. Many varieties are sold sealed so that once they are laid down no further work is required. Others may need periodic varnishing to keep the surface in good order.

RIGHT *The main advantage of a laminate floor is that it blends well with other finishes in a kitchen, and as such can be used specifically to achieve a well-integrated scheme of kitchen design.*

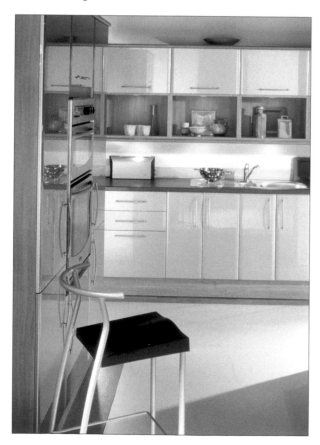

vinyl

Since vinyl is laid down in sheet form, with the entire floor surface of the kitchen often covered by just a single piece, it provides an impenetrable barrier that prevents spillages from reaching the subfloor below. Vinyl is thus exceptionally easy to keep clean and provides a slightly softer and warmer feel underfoot compared to hard tiles or laminate floors. A wide choice of thicknesses and colours are available – as a general rule, the thicker the vinyl the better its quality.

LEFT *The wide variety of patterns and colours means that vinyl can be chosen to suit the overall appearance of most kitchen designs. Here a plain, cool-coloured vinyl has been combined with a laminate trim around units.*

hard tiles

As you would expect, hard tiles are extremely durable and give a definite solid edge to floor finishing. A hard tile floor always creates a dramatic statement in kitchen surroundings and acts well to set off units, producing an ideal foundation for the general appearance of a kitchen. Quality varies according to the thickness of the tiles, and some tiles may require sealing before and after being laid.

soft tiles

Soft tiles cross the boundary between hard tile floors and vinyl. Although they provide the look of hard tiles, and are laid with a similar order of work, soft tiles offer the same qualities of finish as a sheet vinyl floor. If you want the appearance of hard tiles but the warmth and softness underfoot of vinyl, then this option is ideal.

ABOVE *Hard tiles can be laid in traditional designs or offset in a brick bond pattern for an alternative effect. However the tiles are laid, their durable finish is ideal for kitchen floors.*

RIGHT *Painted floorboards provide a wonderfully textured finish, which blends particularly well with kitchen designs that are striving to achieve a more traditional feel.*

BELOW *As long as they are laid correctly, soft tiles provide all the advantages demonstrated by a sheet vinyl floor and are suitable for the majority of kitchens.*

wooden floorboards

Wooden floorboards or planking can offer both an economic and effective choice of kitchen flooring. By using existing or original floorboards, it is simply a case of preparing the surface and applying the correct paint, stain and/or varnish to produce an appealing and durable end product. Although periodic recoating may be necessary to maintain the quality of the finish, floorboards represent an attractive option especially when your budget is tight.

laying a subfloor

Before flooring can be laid in a kitchen, the subfloor will need to be prepared so that it is suitable for receiving the chosen covering. In most homes, subfloors are either wooden based, comprising traditional floorboards or other boards such as chipboard, or composed from a solid concrete base.

concrete subfloors

The amount of preparation required for a concrete subfloor will vary according to the chosen flooring material. If hard tiles are being laid the concrete screed does not need to be as smooth as for vinyl. Although it is always advisable to apply a self-levelling compound to rough concrete floors, with hard tiles it may be enough simply to remove high points and fill holes.

tools for the job

protective equipment

club hammer & bolster chisel

pointing trowel

paintbrush

bucket

power drill & mixing attachment

plastering trowel

1 Knock off any high points on the concrete surface using a club hammer and bolster chisel. Wear gloves and goggles to protect yourself from flying debris.

2 Fill any large depressions with a mortar mix or self-levelling compound mixed to a stiff consistency.

3 Thoroughly sweep the floor clean, then apply a coat of pva solution (1 part pva to 5 parts water) to seal the concrete surface.

tips of the trade

Any traces of bitumen from previous floor coverings will react with the self-levelling compound and adhesives to prevent the new floor material from being laid satisfactorily. Either ensure all traces of bitumen are removed or apply a proprietary sealer.

4 When the pva solution has dried completely, mix up a quantity of self-levelling compound according to the manufacturer's specifications. This can be done by hand, but the easiest way is to use a mixing attachment in conjunction with a power drill.

safety advice

To avoid splashing yourself with the self-levelling compound, the drill must be both started up and switched off only when the mixing attachment is inside the bucket and below the surface level of the compound.

5 Pour the mixed compound immediately across the floor surface and smooth with a plastering trowel. After a little encouragement with the trowel, the self-levelling structure of the compound will take effect, forming a perfectly level surface. Leave to dry overnight, then sand any rough areas before proceeding to lay your chosen floor covering.

tools for the job

claw hammer

cordless drill/driver

craft knife

straight edge

Hard tiles will not tolerate any flexibility in a wooden subfloor and although vinyl has more 'give', any small imperfections in the subfloor surface will show through on the laid vinyl. The best way to achieve a smooth and rigid wooden subfloor is to cover old floorboards with building boards, such as hardboard.

laying hardboard

1 It is generally easiest to work with 120 x 60cm (4 x 2ft) sheets of hardboard as they are easier to handle than larger pieces. Staple or nail them to the existing floorboards at 10cm (4in) centres.

4 Remove the plinth from units and extend the hardboard underneath slightly. This will allow flooring to be extended under the units for a neat finish. The gap under the plinth should be able to accommodate the thickness of the subfloor and flooring (see pages 62–3).

preparing the floor

1 Remove any old or broken nails from the existing floor. A claw hammer is usually the ideal tool to lever out such old fixings.

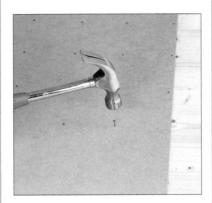

2 Butt join sheets together so that the joints between subsequent rows will be staggered.

85

2 Use normal screws to fix down any loose boards, ensuring that the screws bind tightly with the joists below floor level.

safety advice

Take care not to damage any supply pipes or cables when fixing into the floor. Use a joist/cable detector to help prevent accidents occuring.

3 To cut the hardboard, simply score a line across the surface with a craft knife, then pick up the board and break it along the line.

BOARD TYPES

● **Hardboard** – This is supplied in two different forms: standard and flooring grade. Flooring grade is slightly more expensive but provides a sounder, more rigid subfloor base. Standard hardboard may need to be soaked prior to fitting.

● **Ply** – Thicker than hardboard, the extra rigidity of ply may be required to maintain the surface of hard tile floors. Ply is fitted using a similar method as for hardboard, but the sheets are generally bigger and will need to be cut with a jigsaw or panel saw. If laying hard tiles, the ply should have a minimum thickness of 12mm (½in).

laying vinyl

The combination of softness and durability makes sheet vinyl a popular choice for kitchen floors. Successfully laying vinyl is by no means a simple task, however, especially when cutting the vinyl to fit as there is minimal room for error. It is therefore necessary to take a great deal of time in both the planning and laying of this type of flooring. Higher quality vinyl tends to be thicker, which makes it more difficult to lay, although the finished product is appreciably superior.

Vinyl should always be laid on a subfloor of either hardboard or ply, which must be thoroughly cleaned prior to laying the vinyl to prevent dust or grit from digging into the underside. Vinyl flooring can be fitted before the kitchen units are installed, but this runs the risk of tearing the vinyl during construction and will result in a lot of wastage. It is therefore best to cut around units, leaving sufficient excess so that the vinyl will run slightly underneath once laid. As with tiling, however, if units are free-standing or do not include any plinth then the vinyl will need to be fitted before positioning units.

tips of the trade

• Vinyl becomes more pliable in warm temperatures, so always heat up the room before fitting.

• One of the most difficult aspects of laying vinyl is to achieve an accurate crease. A good trick is to warm the vinyl along junctions with the aid of a hairdryer. This increases the flexibility of the vinyl making it easier to trim into the junction.

• Change craft knife or trimmer blades regularly, as once they have been blunted they can tear the vinyl rather than provide a precise cut.

tools for the job

pencil

scissors

bolster chisel & craft knife
or vinyl trimmer

1 Use old newspaper or lining paper to create a template of the kitchen floor. Roll the paper out and join it with masking tape, allowing it to lip up the skirting or wall surface slightly. Crease around this junction, and make a pencil guideline to show the exact position of the floor/skirting junction. Cut along this line around the entire template perimeter to provide a replica of the floor size.

2 Tape the template to the vinyl and carefully cut the vinyl around the template leaving an excess of 5cm (2in) for final fitting. If the vinyl has a geometric pattern, align the template to ensure the pattern will be suitably positioned. You will find

the procedure easier if the vinyl is rolled out in a separate room, so that the template may be applied when the sheet is totally flat.

3 Having cut the vinyl to size, roll it out in the kitchen allowing the excess to overlap up the skirting/wall junction. Try to make a slight crease in the vinyl along this junction so that it stays in position.

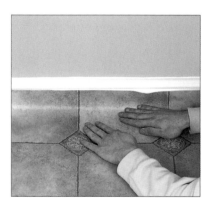

4 Cut the vinyl to fit by first pressing it firmly into the skirting/floor junction with the aid of a bolster chisel, then trimming along the bolster blade with a craft knife. Gradually work your way along each junction trimming as precisely as possible.

SPECIALIST TRIMMERS

Specialist vinyl trimmers are available to buy that crease the vinyl in position while you cut along the junction.

5 Adhesive may be used to secure vinyl, but often heavy-duty vinyls do not need to be stuck down at all. Here double-sided tape has been used around the edge. Pull back the edge of the vinyl, apply tape to the subfloor around the skirting junction, then remove the backing and press the vinyl firmly into place.

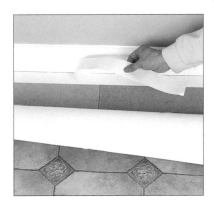

6 Trim back the vinyl underneath the units, cutting around the legs. The aim is to achieve a neat and watertight fit with the plinth.

7 In particularly large rooms, you may need to lay two sheets of vinyl in order to cover the floor. The join between the two sheets will be an area that is potentially prone to becoming unfixed. It is therefore important to secure the edges very firmly to the subfloor. Tape may be used, but ordinary or spray adhesive offers a more hardwearing bond. Pull back the sheets and apply adhesive directly to the subfloor along the join.

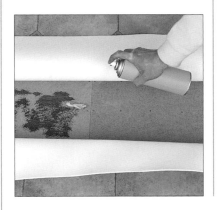

8 Press the two sheets back into position to form a perfect butt join. It is best to join two factory cut edges, as these will be more accurate than those you have cut yourself.

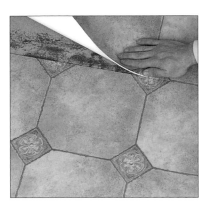

Vinyl provides an attractive finish to a kitchen floor that is both long lasting and easy to clean. It is possible to choose vinyl that mimics other finishes, such as a tiled floor.

laying tiles

Planning where to position each tile involves the same technique for hard and soft tiles alike, but there are marked differences in floor preparation and the type of adhesives used. Hard tiles may be laid on a smooth concrete screed or one that has had self-levelling compound applied. Wooden floors will also accept hard tiles, provided a ply subfloor has first been laid to create a rigid surface. Soft tiles are ideally laid on top of a hardboard or ply subfloor.

planning where to start

It is not normally an option to begin with full tiles along a skirting/wall junction, because slight imperfections in the trueness of wall alignment will become magnified as the tile design progresses. You will therefore need to determine the centre point of the room first and plan out your tiling design from this point.

1 Attach a chalk line between opposing walls, pull it taut and snap the line onto the floor surface to provide a guideline.

2 Repeat this process on the remaining two walls. Where the lines bisect each other is the central point of the room.

3 Starting from this central point, lay tiles out 'dry' working towards the longest wall furthest from the kitchen units.

4 Draw a further guideline to show the starting line for the first full row of tiles. This line should be adjusted to create what will be balanced cuts around the edge of the room.

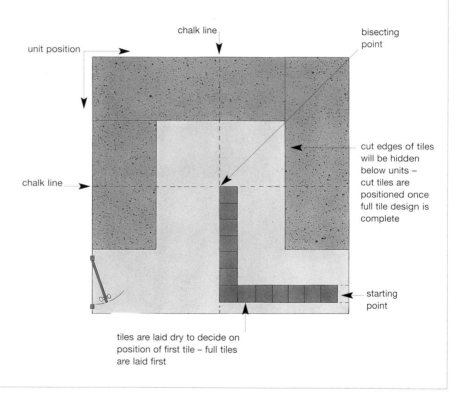

tiles are laid dry to decide on position of first tile – full tiles are laid first

Diagram labels: unit position · chalk line · bisecting point · chalk line · cut edges of tiles will be hidden below units – cut tiles are positioned once full tile design is complete · starting point

TILING BEFORE FITTING

It is possible to lay a tile floor before units have been fixed in place. This provides an ideal level surface for the units but will result in significant wastage of tiles as many will never be seen. However, if your kitchen comprises free-standing units or there is no plinth attached to the base of the units, it will certainly be necessary to tile before fitting the kitchen.

laying hard tiles

Hard tiles are generally laid with a standard floor tile adhesive, but for more heavy-duty varieties, as shown in this example, a mortar mix is often recommended by manufacturers. Floor tiles that are supplied unglazed should be sealed before they are laid, otherwise mortar or grout may become ingrained in their surface during the laying process, which would be difficult to remove later.

tools for the job

tape measure & pencil

chalk line

notched spreader

spirit level

tile cutter

grout spreader & brick jointer

1 Having worked out your starting point following the diagram and instructions above, begin to lay the

first row of tiles along the starting guideline. It is well worth securing a wooden batten along the guideline to provide a good edge to butt the tiles up against. Apply the mortar with a notched spreader in the area where the first tiles are to be laid.

2 Position the first tile allowing it to bed into the mortar until firmly in place. It is vital to get the position of the first tile correct as all the other tiles will follow its lead.

3 Continue to add tiles, making regular checks with a spirit level to ensure that all surfaces are flush,

with no tile edges protruding above surface level or sinking below. Spacers can be used to maintain gaps between tiles, but with the type of tiles shown here judging by 'eye' can provide a less uniform and more pleasingly random appearance.

4 Once all the full tiles have been laid, cut and fit the edge tiles. Thick floor tiles such as those shown should always be cut using an electrically operated tile cutter.

5 The final stage in the process of laying a tile floor is to grout the tiles. Most floor tiles are grouted in a similar way to wall tiles, except heavy-duty varieties, which require a more coarse mixture. Form neat junctions in the grout with a brick jointer.

laying soft tiles

Soft tiles can be laid with adhesive but varieties are also available with a self-adhesive backing. Tiles with backing are far easier to use and

not as messy to work with compared to standard varieties. To establish the starting point for laying soft tiles, employ the same method as for hard tiles, demonstrated opposite.

tools for the job

tape measure & pencil

chalk line

craft knife

straight edge

1 Remove the self-adhesive backing paper from the first tile and position it at the starting point, pressing down firmly onto the subfloor. Continue to add tiles building up the design and butting edges together to form a completely waterproof surface.

2 Fill in the cutting requirement once all the full tiles are laid. Cut soft tiles with a straight edge and craft knife, taking care not to damage the surface below.

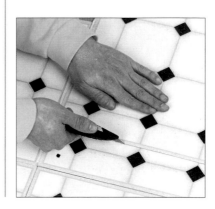

laying a laminate floor ⁊⁊⁊

Laminate floor design has greatly improved in terms of the ease of laying and in its effectiveness as a hardwearing option, though it is always important to check that the variety chosen is suitable for use in a kitchen environment. The more traditional types of laminate board involve gluing joints, but varieties are now available to buy that simply clip together. Boards vary in size according to manufacturer, with an average length of 90cm (3ft).

planning where to start

1 If possible start laying boards against the longest wall, furthest from the units, as it is best not to begin with the process of cutting and trimming. With a laminate floor it is less noticeable if the walls are not perfectly square, hence a skirting board or wall/floor junction is an acceptable starting point.

2 If there are major undulations in the wall surface, you may need to offset the starting line to achieve a more balanced effect.

3 Lay one row at a time across the floor surface.

4 Stagger joints to form a brick bond pattern – this adds strength and improves the appearance.

cuts are hidden below units

underlay laid before laminate boards

starting line

spacers used between wall and board junction – once the floor is complete, spacers are removed and a cover strip applied

joints are staggered

Laminate floors can be laid onto concrete as long as it is totally dry – the manufacturer may also stipulate applying a plastic membrane before laying the floor. Laminate floors can also be laid over any type of wooden floor, as shown in this example.

tools for the job

tape measure

jigsaw

hammer

knocking block

mitresaw

MEMBRANE OPTION

If a plastic membrane is required, skirting must be removed so that the membrane overlaps up the wall surface. Replace the skirting once the floor is laid.

1 Roll out the underlay to cover the floor surface – this provides an even, soundproof cushion. Butt join the edges of subsequent rolls.

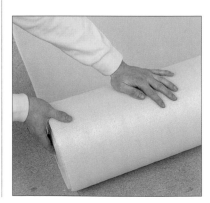

2 For the first row of flooring, use a jigsaw to trim off the back edge or 'tongue' of the boards so that they fit precisely along the wall edge.

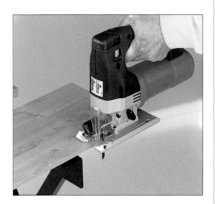

3 Start the second row with a cut board to initiate staggered joints. Address the length to the previous row, overlapping the groove of one board with the tongue of the other.

4 Snap the length into position to lock the board in place.

5 Position spacers on the side wall to maintain a consistent gap around the edge of the boards.

6 Add the next length. To make a butt join, tap the board into place with a hammer and knocking block.

7 Once several rows have been joined, push the floor tight up against the wall, maintaining the perimeter gap with spacers.

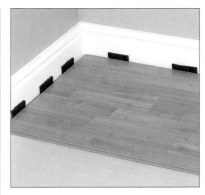

8 Continue laying rows of laminate lengths until the floor is covered, then remove all the spacers and apply a cover strip around the skirting board junction. Cover strips will either be self-adhesive, as shown, or will need to be nailed in place. Mitre the corners for a neat finish.

Laminate floors are easy to lay and provide an impressive, durable finish.

wooden floorboards ↗↗

Wooden planking using the original floorboards can offer an economic yet highly effective kitchen floor surface. The quality of the finish will depend upon the amount of preparation. New floorboards provide an ideal starting surface for the addition of finishing coats. Older boards with previous coatings need to be stripped back to the bare wood before applying a new finish.

preparing a wooden floor

By far the easiest and quickest method for stripping floorboards is to use an electrically-powered machine sander. These machine sanders may be hired relatively cheaply from trade outlets or specialist hire shops. In addition to the basic floor sander, it is also well worth hiring both an edging sander and a corner sander, which will enable you to gain access to all floorboarded areas and not just the central part of the floor.

✋ safety advice

Sanders should always be supplied with instructions for use and relevant safety guidelines. Even if you have used sanders before, always follow the guidelines and instructions very carefully, as there can be slight differences in the operating systems employed by different types of sander. In any event, a dust mask, ear defenders and goggles should always be worn when sanding, as it is both a messy and noisy job.

tools for the job

hammer & nail punch
screwdriver
dust mask
ear defenders
goggles
floor sander
edging sander
corner sander

1 Before you begin to sand the floorboards, it is important to ensure that any nail or screw heads standing proud of the floor are knocked into the surface or just below surface level. Knocking in the nail head with a hammer and nail punch is the best technique. If you leave any heads exposed they could snag and tear the sandpaper on the electric sander. Sanders are generally hired on a flat rate daily basis, but usually the amount of sandpaper you use is charged as extra. Wasting sheets by tearing them on nails can therefore become quite an expensive mistake.

2 With the electric sander unplugged from the mains supply, attach the sandpaper to the custom-made roller mechanism at the base of the machine. The ends of the paper slot behind a metal bar, which is then tightened in place with screws. It is best to start sanding with a coarse grade of paper and gradually reduce the coarseness as you complete sweeps of the floor. Finish off with fine grade paper.

3 Start up the sander tilted back slightly, so that the roller begins moving before you lower it onto the floor surface – if the roller is already touching the floor it can cut into the wood and badly scar the surface. To produce the most even finish, first run the sander diagonally across the floor at a 45°-angle to the direction of the boards. Turn around and repeat the sweep in the opposite direction. Go over the entire floor with diagonal sweeps, then finish by sanding along the boards in the direction of the grain. Remember to change sandpaper and reduce coarseness as required.

4 Use an edging sander to sand flush against the edge of the room. The sanding pad on an edging sander works in an orbital motion, so that the rounded edge allows the sander right up close to the skirting board. The sandpaper is again locked in position on the base with a securing nut. As before, the grade of paper may be reduced in coarseness as the older layers of varnish and stain are sanded away.

5 A corner sander is ideal for getting right into the corner junctions of a room where the edging sander's access is restricted. The pointed edge of these sanders allows for such detailed access. These hand-held sanders are also useful for areas where the staining is particularly stubborn or highly ingrained, particularly in small depressions that the larger sanders may pass over.

6 Sweep up the dust, then wipe over the floor with a cloth dampened in white spirit to pick up the finest dust residue. The floor is now ready for a decorative coating.

finishing the floor

Paint, stain and varnish are just a few of the finishes that may be considered. The kitchen is a hardworking area of the home and the floor requires a hardwearing finish. Always choose good quality materials specifically designed for floor finishing.

tools for the job

paintbrushes

sealant gun

applying stain and varnish

Thoroughly brush out the stain following the direction of the grain with each stroke. Paint each board separately to avoid overlap of stain. Apply at least two coats.

Apply two coats of varnish to the floor surface, whether pre-stained or applying direct. Follow the grain and evenly brush out the varnish.

applying paint

1 Before applying paint, use a sealant gun to fill large cracks or gaps between boards with caulk.

2 Wipe away excess caulk with a damp sponge. Clean the sponge regularly to stop it from clogging.

3 Apply the paint when the caulk is completely dry. There is no need to follow the wood grain but try to brush the paint out evenly. Most floor paint systems require either a primer coat followed by two top coats or simply two or three top coats.

finishing touches

With any room renovation, final touches lend the stamp of professionalism to a competent construction job. To achieve a harmonious look the various elements comprising a kitchen will need to receive some degree of decoration, with careful attention given to colour schemes, window dressing and methods of finishing surfaces. Additional storage features should also be considered, both to serve a practical purpose and add interest to the room. This chapter examines the different options available for decoration and additional storage, and provides instruction on the techniques required to achieve the best possible finish.

Only the splashback area for the hob has been tiled, creating a decorative feature that blends beautifully with the walls.

options for finishing

Kitchen finishing is an area that includes not only the normal decorative aspects associated with finishing a room, but also the addition of practical features that can help the kitchen to function at a maximum level of efficiency. Choice in this area is particularly wide and varied, so it is important to take some time when making your decisions.

shelving

Of all the rooms in a house the kitchen has perhaps the greatest practical requirements, and one key aspect is the provision of adequate storage areas. Kitchen units themselves will generally provide all the hidden storage you require, but it is still likely that you will need to make use of some open storage areas in the form of shelving. As well as offering ease of access to frequently used foodstuffs or equipment, open shelving can also serve an aesthetic purpose and be used for decorative display. Contemporary shelving design offers considerable choice, and methods for fixing and securing shelves onto the wall surface are similarly varied.

RIGHT *Shelves take many forms and can either be tied in with other kitchen surfaces by employing the same finish as for the worktop, or they can be made to contrast. The addition of hooks to these shelves provides extra storage.*

window dressing

Although this area can often be neglected, like all rooms in the house kitchens require some form of window dressing in the form of curtains or blinds. Indeed, deciding how to dress the windows of a kitchen potentially offers a highly creative avenue for producing a decorative finish. Blinds are a particularly popular choice as they make the best use of space and allow the most light into the room when opened. Curtains are another suitable option but they are likely to take up more space and therefore hanging them requires greater consideration. In addition, with all the food preparation and cooking activity undertaken in a kitchen it is important to consider the ease with which curtain material or blinds may be cleaned and secured out of the way.

LEFT *In a kitchen with relatively simple decoration, a patterned blind can be used to add a splash of colour and to create a more comfortable and welcoming atmosphere.*

tiling

Tiles are frequently used to form a splashback area in kitchens because they combine the qualities of durability, ease of cleaning and attractive decoration. Kitchen tiles are available in a vast range of colours, offering ample scope to complement or contrast with units, while patterned or relief tiles offer a further option by introducing a more textured or three-dimensional finish. As long as they are carefully applied and properly grouted and sealed, tiles represent an effective choice for finishing in many kitchens.

worktops

Applying a finish to a wooden worktop is essential to seal and protect the wood, thereby increasing its hardwearing capabilities. There are different types of oil available for this purpose and a finish may be chosen according to personal preference. Or you might like to create a tiled worktop, which, though harder work, offers greater scope for decoration with the possibility of choosing coloured and patterned tiles.

ABOVE *The tiles in this kitchen help to pick out the colour of both the units and worktop, creating a truly dramatic look and making a definite contribution to the fitted effect.*

LEFT *Natural wood tends to blend well with most kitchen surfaces, whether they be painted or of a similar natural finish.*

BELOW *In a room with a high ceiling, a suspended ceiling storage system makes perfect sense because it utilizes what would otherwise be redundant space and also produces a strong visual impact.*

ceiling storage

Ceiling storage refers to the use of ceilings for suspending storage systems, which offers an alternative way of keeping items and a good method for saving space. Many systems of fixing can be used to suspend ceiling storage – brackets, chains, hooks and 'eyes' are all acceptable options provided secure fixings are made, which can generally be achieved by inserting the fixings into ceiling joists.

fitting shelving ↗↗

Kitchen shelves are usually fitted to provide storage in addition to wall units. Where budgets are limited, however, shelves can be used as a straight alternative to wall units, and in small kitchens where space is at a premium and wall units would create a rather cramped atmosphere, simple shelving is a suitable option. Whatever your reasons may be for choosing to install shelving, it is vital to employ adequate fixing techniques to ensure the shelves are level and secure enough to support weight requirements.

making use of worktop

A good way of making use of the inevitable leftover pieces of worktop is to make extra shelving. Moreover, the width and depth of worktop material allows for hidden fixings.

tools for the job

tape measure & pencil

jigsaw or panel saw

cordless drill/driver

router (optional)

hacksaw

disposable resin applicator

1 Mark the outline of the shelf on the worktop. Then cut around this guideline – a jigsaw is ideal for this purpose but you can also use a panel saw. Using a flathead bit, drill holes at a point outside the guideline to accommodate the jigsaw blade. A router may be used to shape a decorative moulded edge around the front of the shelf if desired (see page 57 for further instructions).

2 Firmly clamp the cut-out shelf to a workbench and use a drill with a flat bit to make two holes in the back edge of the shelf, relatively close to either end. The holes need to be just wider than the circumference of a threaded bolt, which will be used as the wall fixing mechanism.

3 Cut the two bolts to length using a hacksaw. The bolts should penetrate inside the shelf to a depth of at least half the shelf width, and should penetrate into the wall to an equal distance. Measure and mark off the position of the holes on the wall, checking they are aligned, and drill the holes required.

4 Insert resin into the holes in the wall with the disposable applicator. Push the threaded bolts into the holes and allow the resin to dry out. Once the bolts are secured, use the applicator to insert resin into the bolt holes in the shelf itself.

5 Lift the shelf into position fitting the holes in the back edge over the threaded bolts in the wall.

tips of the trade

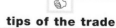

Resin drying times will vary. Follow the guidelines to ensure you get the timing right when making the fixing.

hidden fixing brackets

The more traditional approach to fitting shelves involves a visible bracket, but it is still possible to hide the fixings. Once again, discarded worktop may be used to create the shelving.

1 Again, measure and mark the outline of the shelf on the worktop. Use this guideline to cut the worktop to size, ideally using a jigsaw but otherwise a panel saw will be adequate. Drill holes outside the guideline for initially inserting the jigsaw blade. Having cut the shelf you may turn your attention to attaching the hidden brackets. Hold the housing section of one of the brackets against the wall and employ a mini level to ensure that it is precisely vertical. Then mark the fixing position with a bradawl.

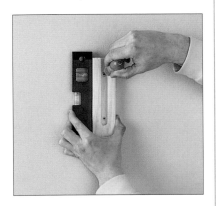

2 Drill the correct size of hole in the wall and fit wall plugs. They may push in by hand, or require some additional encouragement with one or two taps of the butt end of a hammer.

3 Now reposition the housing section and screw it securely in place. Check it once more with a mini level to ensure that it has not shifted out of position.

4 Position the second housing section on the wall next to the section already fixed in place. It will need to be positioned at the correct distance to accommodate the shelf. Place a spirit level across the top of both sections to ensure that they are precisely level and aligned. Once again mark with a bradawl through the second section to indicate where you need to screw.

5 Screw the section in place, then slide the support brackets into both the housing sections.

6 Finally, position the shelf and secure it in place by using a hammer to knock one or two panel pins through the top of the shelf and into the brackets below.

ALTERNATIVE SHELVING SYSTEMS

In both the examples shown, leftover wooden worktop has been used to create extra shelving, thereby helping to create an overall integrated look to the kitchen. However, most DIY outlets will stock a wide selection of shelving systems, and you may prefer to choose a material or design that provides a contrast with the other kitchen surfaces. Whatever system you ultimately choose, the secret of successful shelving remains the same – make sure the shelves sit level and that the brackets and fixings will be able to bear the weight requirements.

fitting ceiling & peninsula storage

Ceiling and peninsula storage makes use of areas other than those around the perimeter of a kitchen. The process of fitting such storage systems must wait until all other fixtures have been installed. For example, a peninsula unit can only be fitted after the worktop is in place.

ceiling storage

The most important consideration when fitting any system of ceiling storage is to ensure adequate fixings are made. The fixing mechanism must be secure enough to support the combined weight of the storage system itself and the foodstuffs or equipment that will be stored in it. To achieve this, not only does the mechanism need to be strong enough, but the fixings must normally be made at points in the wall corresponding to joist position. You will therefore need to locate the joist positions for planning purposes. A joist detector is the ideal tool for this task, enabling decisions to be made on where items such as airers or proprietary hanging racks can be situated. Sometimes there may have to be a compromise between the ideal location for such a system and the actual position of the joists. However, because joists will always run parallel, it means that fixings may be inserted in positions that will result in a 'square' or aligned appearance.

safety advice

When fixing into ceilings, care must be taken to ensure that supply pipes or cables are not damaged. Therefore, as well as locating joists it is essential to use a pipe and cable detector as well, in order to avoid accidents.

peninsula storage

Some peninsula units are fixed at ceiling level, especially in kitchens with low ceilings. Or they may also be held in place by a supportive framework and pole. This latter type of support system is shown in the following example, which demonstrates a standard technique for securing these type of units in place. Since peninsula units tend to form a focal point in the kitchen and are viewed from more than one side, it is important to adhere to the correct installation procedure and to ensure levels are checked repeatedly to make certain the end product looks as impressive as possible.

tools for the job

tape measure

pencil &/or chinagraph

cordless drill/driver

Allen key

hacksaw

adjustable spanner

1 Measure up from the top edge of the worktop and mark on the wall the position of the fixing bracket for the peninsula framework. Height may be dictated by other units in the kitchen, otherwise the supporting pole supplied will act as a rough guide – 40–45cm (16–18in) is a good average height. When you mark the bracket

position remember to account for the need to align the back edge of the peninsula units with those below.

2 Position the wall bracket at the marked-off point, holding a mini level on top of it to ensure precise levelling. Mark off fixing points through the holes in the bracket.

3 With some designs, the bracket is then fixed to the wall and the supportive framework attached to it. For this example, you first need to attach some fixing brackets to the wall bracket. Screw the fixing brackets using an Allen key.

4 Now fix the wall bracket to the
main supporting framework
using the Allen key.

5 The next stage is to fix the
supportive leg to the other
end of the framework, but before
doing so position any washers or
other fixing details according to the
manufacturer's guidelines.

6 Enlist a helper to hold up the
framework from the wall bracket
position, allowing the supporting pole
to rest on the worktop surface. Take
time to ensure that the pole is centrally
positioned and correctly aligned with
the wall bracket. Draw around the
supportive pole to mark its position.

A normal pencil may be used for this
purpose, but with darker worktops a
chinagraph will make guidelines as
clear as possible.

7 Remove the entire framework
and drill a hole through the
centre of the guideline around the
supporting pole. Remember to choose
a drill bit that corresponds to the size
of bolt supplied for fixing the pole.

8 Reposition the entire peninsula
framework and secure the wall
bracket in place by drilling and
screwing through the holes marked
off in step 2.

9 Fix the pole bolt through the
drilled hole into the base of
the pole. Tighten with a spanner
so it cannot shift out of position.

10 Fix the units onto the
framework by screwing up
through the underside of the frame
into the unit. To join the units once
positioned, follow the same technique
described in steps 8 and 9 on pages
52–3. You should also fix through
the end unit into the wall surface.

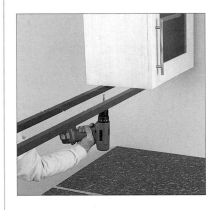

11 Apply cornice at the top and
a pelmet strip at the base of
the units to disguise the framework.

finishing a wooden worktop ⌐

Unlike its laminate alternative, wooden worktop requires some form of finishing to seal the grain once it has been fitted. Wood oils generally achieve the best results and although periodic maintenance coats will need to be reapplied, this is a much easier method of renewing the look of the worktop than stripping and applying a polyurethane varnish – damaged areas can also be repaired with a higher level of success (see page 114). As such, the worktop can almost be treated like a piece of furniture that gains character and mellows in appearance with age.

tools for the job

protective equipment

sandpaper &/or electric sander

oil brush

cloths

1 Wood oils can damage other kitchen surfaces, so before beginning any work it is vital to mask all other areas near the worktop to protect them from any spillages or overspray. Pay special attention to the front of the base units where drips or runs from the edge of the worktop are most likely to fall. Tape a plastic sheet across the front of the units to protect them. Some types of vinyl flooring may be highly susceptible

to staining from certain wood treatments, so cover the floor with dust sheets before starting work.

2 Although wooden worktop is supplied with a relatively smooth surface, it will still need some honing with sandpaper to remove any rough areas. In this case the sanding has been done by hand, but you can also use an electric sander to speed things up. Always sand in line with the wood grain and be careful not to scratch fittings such as sink edges or hobs.

3 Take particular care sanding in line with the grain next to joints, as this is where the grain is likely to

run in two different directions. Attention to this sort of detail will show in the finished product.

4 If you have used a router along the front edge of the worktop, it may have left the occasional scorch mark – this can occur if too much time is spent dwelling in one position when the router is moved along the worktop edge. These darkened areas will show up through an oiled surface, so it is vital to sand the area until the burn mark is removed.

5 After you have given the whole worktop a thorough sanding, clean away the worst of the debris with a dusting brush, and then wipe the whole surface down with a cloth dampened in white spirit. The white spirit will remove even the finest dirt particles from the worktop and will evaporate quickly to leave a totally dust-free surface. Wear gloves to protect your hands.

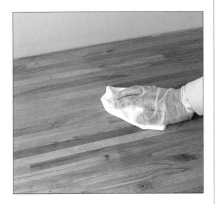

6 Give the wood oil a thorough stir then generously apply it to the worktop. Brush with the grain, allowing the oil to spread across the entire worktop surface.

7 Allow the oil to soak into the wood surface, before removing

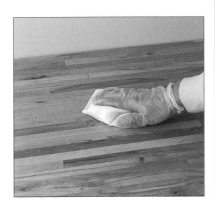

any excess pools of oil with a dry cloth. At the same time, buff the surface to produce a dull shine.

8 Wipe off any overspill onto metal surfaces before it dries. Allow the oil to dry overnight, then repeat the process with at least three coats.

VARNISH OILING

Oiling a worktop with the technique demonstrated here provides a fairly dull matt finish. A greater sheen may be gained by applying the oil with a brush and not rubbing away the excess. This coats the wood in the direction of the grain, treating the oil more like a varnish. The only drawbacks with this technique is that the oil takes a lot longer to dry, and if the worktop is not totally dust-free the finish will have a gritty appearance. Therefore, before each new application of oil, give the surface a light sand and then use a cloth dampened in white spirit to wipe over the worktop to provide a totally dust-free surface.

The natural grain and colouring of a wooden worktop makes an attractive surface in almost any kitchen design – an oil finish will seal and enhance the look of the wood.

tiling walls ⚒⚒⚒

The area covered when tiling walls in a kitchen is usually rather small and tends to be restricted to the wall space immediately above the worktop, with the number of rows limited to the distance between the surface of the worktop and the wall units. Even if there are no wall units, the tile level need not extend too high since its main function is to act as a splashback. The only major obstacles to overcome are corners and socket outlets common in the area above a worktop.

👍 tips of the trade

• **Where to start** – Always begin at the opposite end to any corners that will need tiling around, that way the cut tiles will be in the corner and less obvious to the eye. You should also consider how best to centralize a hob or sink unit within the tile design.

• **Keeping clean** – Have a bucket of warm water and a sponge to hand at all times. Keeping your hands and tools as clean as possible will make the job much easier.

• **After oiling** – If you are applying tiles above a wooden worktop, it is best to apply the oil finish to the worktop first (see pages 102–3). Otherwise tile adhesive or grout may become ingrained in the wood, causing needless extra preparation before the surface can be oiled. Oiling seals the wood surface so the wet adhesive and grout can simply be wiped off with a damp sponge.

• **Wall surfaces** – Walls must first be prepared so that they are in a sound condition to receive the adhesive. Before application, therefore, remove wallpaper, fill any holes and seal dusty surfaces with a coat of pva solution (1 part pva to 5 parts water).

tools for the job

tape measure

notched spreader

felt tip pen

tile cutter or cutting machine

grout spreader

grout shaper

bucket

sponge

general technique

1 Apply adhesive to the wall, covering an area no larger than 1 sq.m (1sq.yd) – any larger and the adhesive will dry before you can apply all the tiles. Use a notched spreader to provide an even covering. Employ spacers between tiles to maintain even gaps. Lay a row of spacers along the worktop as well to provide an even gap with the first row of tiles.

2 Continue to spread adhesive on the wall and apply tiles, adding further rows, building up the tile design and maintaining consistent gaps with the spacers.

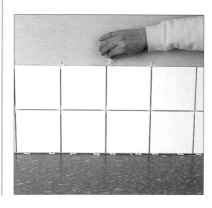

dealing with switches

1 When tiling around electrical sockets or switches, you will need extra time to cut tiles before the adhesive dries, and so you should only apply enough adhesive to the wall to cope with immediate demands. Measure and mark off on the tile the portion that needs to be removed for fitting. A felt tip pen is ideal for making a clear mark on tile surfaces. Release the electrical socket from the wall and measure to accommodate a slight overlap of the tile behind the socket. After the tile has been finished, the socket is then screwed back in place onto the overlapping edge of the tile to form a neat finish.

🖐 safety advice

Always switch off the main power supply before undoing electrical sockets. You may need to use longer retaining screws to hold the socket back in place once the tiling is complete. This is important as it is very dangerous to leave a socket hanging off the wall.

2 An electric tile cutting machine is ideal for cutting a right-angled section, but a manual cutter will suffice. Follow the manufacturer's guidelines for safe use and extend the felt tip marks to provide guidelines for cutting.

3 Apply adhesive to the back of the tile and position it next to the socket. Again, use spacers to maintain the gap with other tiles.

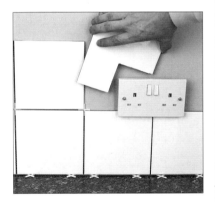

cutting & finishing

1 To make simple straight cuts, a normal tile cutter or tile cutting

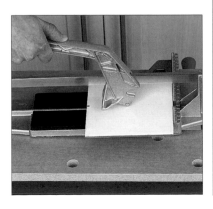

machine may be used. First make a scored line along the tile surface, then press down on the handle of the cutter to break the tile along this scored line.

2 When the design is complete and the adhesive has dried (normally overnight), remove spacers

as necessary before pressing grout with a grout spreader into all the joints between the tiles. Remove any excess grout, then use a grout shaper to further 'tool' and neaten the joints.

3 Finish by polishing the surface with a sponge to reveal a clean and bright tiled surface.

White or pale-coloured tiles are ideal to use below wall units, as their reflective properties will help to brighten the area, making it easier to work in.

tiling a worktop ⚒

A tiled worktop offers a different look and finishing option to the more traditional laminate or wooden alternatives. Depending upon the quality of tiles chosen, it can be an inexpensive way of producing a hardwearing and attractive work surface.

The technique for tiling a worktop is similar to that employed for tiling walls, although some adjustment is needed to produce the best finish. Ensure that the tiles you choose are recommended for use on worktops.

tools for the job

panel saw or jigsaw

clamp

cordless drill/driver

mitresaw

hammer

paintbrush

notched spreader

grout spreader

tile cutter

sponge

cloth

1 The tiles will need to be laid on a solid surface. Plyboard represents the best choice of material for this purpose. Choose ply of at least 12mm (½in) in thickness – any less will be too flexible to form a rigid worktop. Following a similar technique for fitting wooden worktop on pages 56–7, cut the ply to the requisite size.

Leave an overhang at the front of the units, and fix it to the worktop by screwing underneath, through the unit and into the ply. If your kitchen comes with corner fixing blocks, use them for fixing through. Clamp the ply firmly in place so that it is fixed tightly to the units and cannot shift out of position as the screws are inserted.

2 Before tiling, attach a finished edge to the ply. In this example, a hardwood strip is used. Measure the length of the edges and cut strips to size with a mitresaw.

3 Attach the hardwood strips to the edge of the ply with a generous amount of wood glue to ensure a strong adhesive bond.

4 Press the strips in place along the edge of the ply using some of the tiles to help adjust the exact level at which the strip needs to be attached. This is a very important stage of the tiling process, as the ideal finish should allow the top of the tiles to sit absolutely flush with the top of the wooden strip. If the wooden strip is positioned too high, this creates a ridge along the edge of the work surface making it more difficult to wipe down when in use. If necessary, knock one or two panel pins into the strips to hold them in position while the glue dries.

5 Once the adhesive has dried, coat the wooden strips with some protective varnish to seal their surface. If the wood is left unsealed at this stage, when the tiles are grouted some excess may become ingrained in the wood, which will then prove difficult to clean before varnishing. Carrying out the process this way around means that any excess grout will simply wipe clean off the varnished wooden surface of the strips.

6 To ensure the best finish, it is worth laying the tiles out dry before applying any adhesive. By doing this you can plan the design and work out the ideal places to use cut tiles. It is best to begin with full tiles along the front edge of the work surface, so that any cuts can be planned to appear along the back junction with the wall. Likewise, if the work surface includes a corner, as shown here, it is best to start with a full tile in the corner, and build up the rest of the design from this point.

7 To make the tiling easier, apply a coat of pva solution (1 part pva to 5 parts water) to the ply surface. This helps to seal the ply, making it much easier to spread adhesive. Allow the ply to dry before proceeding to tile.

8 Use a notched spreader, ideally a large one, to spread adhesive across the ply surface. Do not spread more than about 1sq.m (1sq.yd) at a time. Use the notches to maintain a consistent depth of adhesive, which helps to ensure a consistent tile level.

9 Apply the tiles, pressing them down into the adhesive with a slight twisting motion. Since the tiles are applied to a horizontal surface there is no risk of them slipping down, which is a major consideration when tiling walls. However, it still pays to be vigilant. If rows of tiles are allowed to go out of 'square', this will effect the finish and lead to some unsightly tile-cutting. You should therefore take time to position the tiles correctly, and use spacers to keep all gaps consistent. Spacers will also be required, albeit temporarily, along the junction between the edge tiles and the wooden edge strip, again to ensure the lines of tiles are kept consistent.

10 Once the adhesive has dried grout the tiled surface with an epoxy grout. This type of grout is more hardwearing than standard grout, and more hygienic for surfaces upon which food will almost certainly be prepared. It is best to concentrate on small areas at a time, since epoxy grout can be difficult to work with and also dries very quickly. Force the grout

firmly into every joint, removing any excess as quickly as possible with a damp sponge.

11 Wait until the grout has completely dried out, then give the tiled surface a final wipe over with a sponge and polish with a cotton cloth. This will help to remove any remaining grout residue leaving a clean and bright, finished surface.

tips of the trade

When grouting tiles on walls, the joints themselves are often tooled with a grout shaper to produce, what are in effect, slightly concave channels between each of the tiles. However, it is best not to apply this particular technique when grouting tiles on the horizontal work surfaces of the kitchen, as it is important to keep the grout level fairly flush with the surface. This technique will make the tiled surface more even overall and, as such, easier to wipe clean in the future. It will also reduce the frequency with which grime or dirt can become trapped along the grout points.

decorative finishing ⤢

Although much of the wall area in a kitchen tends to be covered over by units and accessories, it is still important to choose an attractive decorative scheme for the exposed walls, woodwork and ceiling. Everyone will have their own personal preferences regarding pattern and colour, but to achieve the best results some modifications should be made to the basic techniques for applying paint and wallpaper in order to cope with the specific kitchen environment.

using paint

There are many durable varieties of paint and numerous colours to choose from, and the finish can easily be maintained by simply applying new coats whenever needed. The fitted nature of modern kitchens will require a great deal of 'cutting in', or painting sharp edges and dividing lines between units and walls. As such, it is worth buying quality brushes that make it possible to paint tight up into the edges with accuracy.

You can also apply masking tape to protect surface edges, which can easily be removed once you have completed the job.

Apply hardwearing paint to all kitchen surfaces, so that it can be wiped down and kept clean. For this reason oil-based paints are still commonly used in kitchens. Manufacturers have now developed specialist kitchen paints, however, which although water-based are still highly durable.

using paper

Wallpaper can be used in kitchens, but limit yourself to hardwearing varieties designed for kitchen use. Vinyl papers are ideal and, if applied correctly, should last for many years. Again, because there are so many dividing edges in a kitchen, papering can be quite a complicated and fiddly process. Attention must be focussed on precise cutting in order to achieve the best results.

A kitchen environment is particularly prone to condensation and changes in temperature, and these factors can cause wallpaper to lift or peel away. In some situations it is possible to reduce the chances of this occuring. For example, where wallpaper meets

tiles, apply the paper first so that it lips below what will be the edge of the final row of tiles. When the tiles are fitted they will cover the paper edge, thereby preventing it from peeling at a later date.

Applying varnish or a glaze coat to papers will make them easier to wipe down. With some vinyls, however, varnish will not adhere to the paper surface, so it is always best to try a test patch beforehand.

tips of the trade

• **Masking up** – Always mask up units with plastic sheets to protect their finish, before starting to paint or paper walls.

• **Pre-installation** – Due to the fiddly nature of kitchen decoration, it is worth painting the ceiling and even applying one coat to the walls before the kitchen is installed. This can save a great deal of time when it comes to the finishing process.

• **Ventilation** – Ensure that the kitchen has good ventilation systems as this will lengthen the lifespan of any decorative finish.

sealing junctions

Kitchen surfaces are frequently cleaned and liable to become wet, especially around sinks. As a result, it is vital to take precautions by sealing all areas to prevent the water from penetrating and causing mould or rotting surfaces. Silicone sealants are the most effective way of dealing with the joints between different surfaces as they form both a flexible and waterproof seal. Sealant should be applied at the junction between wallpaper and skirting board, around windows or at the junction between skirting board and a vinyl floor. The area where it is of greatest importance, however, is at the back of a worktop to seal the gap next to the wall. In this example, a seal is made between a laminate worktop and a tiled splashback.

tools for the job

sealant dispenser

craft knife

1 Masking tape will help to produce a neat finish. Apply the tape on either side of the junction, maintaining an even gap between the two strips.

2 Using a craft knife, cut the nozzle off the sealant tube to a diameter slightly greater than that of the gap between the two strips of masking tape.

3 Fit the sealant tube into the dispenser and pull the trigger to expel the sealant. Move the nozzle of the sealant tube along the masked-off junction at a constant but gradual pace, so that an even coverage or 'bead' of sealant is produced.

4 Now smooth down the sealant with a wetted finger in order to create a neat finish.

5 Before the sealant has had time to dry out, very carefully remove the masking tape strips to reveal an exact and evenly proportioned bead of sealant.

6 You may need to make one final smooth with a wetted finger to achieve the best possible finish.

tips of the trade

● **The last job** – Silicone sealant is a particularly difficult substance to work with, as it tends to stick to everything and anything. Once dry its appearance cannot be altered since it is impossible to paint over. It is therefore vital that you make the job of applying sealant the last part of your kitchen renovation.

● **Removing unwanted sealant** – Before the sealant dries it is possible to remove any excess material simply by wiping it away using a cloth dampened in white spirit.

● **Drying times** – Sealant will 'go off' relatively quickly, but it will not have dried out completely for at least 24 hours. You should therefore avoid wiping down the sealant until such time has elapsed.

● **Keeping clean** – Sealant has very strong adhesive qualities, so always keep a ready supply of kitchen towels or cloths at hand, to clean away any excess as you progress with the job.

fitting curtains & blinds

Important factors specific to the kitchen environment will need to be taken into consideration when making your choice of window dressing, but the actual technique for fitting curtains and blinds in a kitchen is no different to any other room.

If the window is positioned above a worktop area then the hanging system and material of the window dressing must occupy the minimum amount of space. Hence voluminous, billowing curtains are clearly not a practical option, as they would encroach too far into the working area. Different systems may be used for different windows in the room. For example, blinds could be fitted in a window above the worktop, with curtains dressing a French window leading to the garden.

tools for the job

tape measure & pencil

straight edge &/or spirit level

cordless drill/driver

screwdriver

curtains

The prevalence of condensation and different fumes in a kitchen can be damaging to many curtain materials. It is thus important to choose a material that is hardwearing and/or washable. Curtains may be hung on either a track or a pole.

curtain tracks

Tracks tend to be regarded as the less attractive type of curtain rail and as such are normally kept discretely hidden by ensuring that the head of the curtain covers the track as much as possible. Tracks represent a good choice where space is limited, however, since they hold the curtain tight against the wall or window.

1 Draw a level guideline above the window to indicate the position of the track. Using a spirit level for a straight edge is the easiest way to ensure a level line. Curtain tracks require frequent fixing points in order to support the curtain weight. Mark off equidistant points along the line and drill and plug these positions.

2 Screw in the brackets along this line making sure the brackets are the right way up and that they bite firmly into the plugged holes.

3 Once all the brackets have been fixed in place, clip the curtain track onto the front of them. You will need to position the track so that it overhangs either side of the window by an equal amount. Now simply fit track gliders and hang the curtain.

curtain poles

A curtain pole offers a more ornate hanging system than tracks. You will usually find that the ends of the pole are embellished with finials, and in many cases the curtain head is deliberately made to hang below the pole so that its decorative qualities are always in view. A major drawback is that a pole will cause the curtain to encroach further into the room, but provided this will not be problematic in terms of the layout of your kitchen, then poles are an ideal choice for hanging curtains.

1 Fit a bracket at each corner of the window to hold the pole in place. For large windows you may

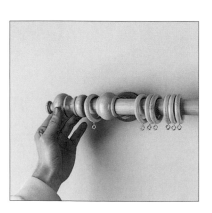

need to fit a central bracket as well. The curtain is usually hung with rings, with a finial attached to both ends of the pole in order to prevent the curtain from falling off.

blinds

Blinds provide probably the most practical option for window dressing in a kitchen. They can be positioned tight up against the window surface to save space, are normally made from an easy-to-clean material, and their adjustable height makes it easy to control light intensity in the room. Blinds are generally supplied in a kit form that involves fixing brackets to the window frame.

1 Measure the width of the window before buying your blind to make sure of the correct requirement. It is very important to take measurements all the way down the window, not just at the top, as distortions in the shape of the recess may result in the window being narrower at the bottom. If there is significant distortion then the blind must be bought with the narrowest measurement in mind so that it will fit comfortably within the window recess.

2 Fit the fixing brackets in the top corners of the window, screwing into the wooden frame. Make sure that each bracket is positioned the correct way up and at the right corner for each end of the blind.

3 Position the roller blind and then insert each end into the correct bracket. You will notice one bracket is of a different shape to the other, as the fittings on each end of the roller are made to fit with only one of the brackets. Finally, attach a cord pull to the blind so that it may be put into operation.

tips of the trade

Blind kits are sometimes supplied with the blind material separate from the roller. Join the blind to the roller with staples, double-sided tape or double-sided velcro, which is useful for taking the blind down again for cleaning.

A blind was the ideal choice of window dressing for this kitchen, as it rests tight against the window frame and does not intrude into the working area of the sink.

repairing a kitchen

No matter how fine the quality of fixtures, fittings and finishes in the kitchen, you will almost certainly need to make repairs at some stage. In most cases the incidence of repairs is determined by frequency of use, but that said, it is not uncommon to find tap washers need changing, door handles fixing or worktops resealing during the lifetime of even relatively underused kitchens. This chapter demonstrates how to make all these repairs and focuses on many other areas in the kitchen that at some stage or another will need to be repaired. It is important to make repairs as soon as the need arises and not to allow the kitchen to fall into neglect, since regular maintenance in the short term helps to extend the life of the kitchen and will save you money in the long term.

All kitchens need repairs over time – with this kitchen, for example, you may need to replace a broken tile on the worktop.

reviving worktop ⁄⁄

Worktops are invariably the most used of all kitchen surfaces and as a consequence will probably require frequent repairs to maintain their condition. Outlined below are a number of common problems experienced with different types of worktop and guidance on the best techniques for returning them to good order.

wooden worktop

Wooden worktop should receive occasional reoiling, but you may also need to make localized repairs caused by spillages that have been allowed to soak in and stain, or through surface scarring caused by knives or other cutting implements.

tools for the job

electric sander (optional)

cloth

1 Sand the affected area until the stain has been removed. An electric sander is ideal for this purpose but take care not to dig the edge into the worktop, which will cause undulations in the wood surface.

2 Apply a small amount of oil to a dry cloth and gently rub it into the sanded area. You may need to make two or three applications to blend the area back in with the existing worktop.

laminate worktop

Damage to a laminate finish cannot be simply sanded away – it is more a case of effective camouflaging.

repairing edges

tools for the job

small fitch

masking tape

1 If the edge has chipped, glue the broken piece of laminate back in position, if possible, using neat pva.

2 Use masking tape to hold the section securely in position while the glue dries.

scratches

tools for the job

artist's brush

dry cloth

1 To deal with surface scratches, simply dust and clean the area then paint along the groove with a fine artist's brush using an oil-based paint such as eggshell. Try and match the worktop colour as closely as possible. For a patterned worktop it is best to choose one of the darkest colours in its design. Wipe away any excess.

repairing the front edge

Where damage to a laminate worktop is so extreme that minor repairs would have little effect, you may need to consider replacing the front edge with an alternative finish. In this example, a wood moulding has been used to create a new decorative edging on the front of the worktop.

tools for the job

clamps

combination square

jigsaw

hammer (optional)

1 Clamp a section of batten along the front edge of the worktop. It needs to be positioned so that a jigsaw can rest against the side, then use the batten for a guide as it is moved along the worktop, producing a straight cut along the edge.

2 Remove the damaged worktop edge with a jigsaw. Keep the blade tight against the batten to make sure of a dead straight cut.

3 Cut and glue a length of moulding along the newly cut edge of the worktop. Fix the moulding

with either wood glue or pva. Nail one or two panel pins through the moulding to hold it in place while the glue dries, if necessary. Stain and varnish the batten to seal the surface and provide a decorative finish.

tiling over

If damage to the worktop is excessive, then a further option is to tile over the entire worktop surface to provide a completely new look.

tools for the job

tiling equipment

1 Attach moulding along the front edge of the worktop, and stain and varnish it to your preference. Then apply tiles directly on top of the worktop (see pages 106–7 for further instructions). Remember that sink or hob height may have to be adjusted so that the tiles can be lipped under the edges of such appliances.

resiliconing

The overall appearance of a worktop can often be let down simply by staining or damage over time to the silicone seal. By periodically replacing the seal, you will not only revive the look of the worktop, but also renew the waterproof seal between the worktop/wall junction.

tools for the job

paintbrush

window scraper

craft knife

sealant dispenser or gun

1 Paint a proprietary sealant removal solution onto the silicone allowing it to soak in as much as possible.

2 Use a window scraper to ease the old seal away. Then clean the area thoroughly before reapplying a new silicone bead (see page 109).

fixing doors & drawers

Hinges and handles on drawers and doors are the areas that most commonly suffer damage on kitchen units. As moving parts, it is inevitable that hinges will eventually wear out and the daily tugging on handles will similarly loosen the fixing or even pull off the handle altogether. In some cases, once these sort of breakages begin to occur it can signal the time for a new kitchen. Generally, however, only the most frequently used doors or drawers in a kitchen will experience any major problems. Fixing such one-off problems can therefore return the kitchen to optimum working level and does not have to signal the need for a complete kitchen refit.

repairing a hinge

tools for the job

cordless drill/driver

pencil

combination square

hinge cutting bit

mini level

A sagging or off-level door will often indicate that there is a problem with hinges. The movement of the hinge is likely to have caused the fixing holes of the hinge plate to widen, so that the plate comes away from the side of the carcass. The best way to fix this problem is to relocate the hinge plate to a slightly higher position on the door, which will require refixing both the plate and hinge mechanism itself.

1 Unscrew the door from the unit and remove both the loose hinge plate from the carcass and the hinge mechanism from the door.

2 Use a combination square to measure up from the original hinge position to a new location further up the door. Mark the central point for the new recess required to house the hinge.

3 The next stage is to cut the new hinge recess in the door. This can be done using a cordless drill by attaching a hinge cutting bit. Make sure that the point of the hinge cutter is precisely inserted at the marked-off point for the centre of the new recess. Gradually cut into the door taking care to drill to the exact depth requirement for the hinge.

4 Thoroughly dust out the hole and then screw the hinge into the new recess, ensuring that it is correctly aligned with the door edge. Before rehanging the door, fill the old recess with matching wood filler.

5 Use the same measurement to mark off on the inside of the carcass the change in position of the hinge plate. Then reattach the hinge plate by screwing it securely in place. Rehang the door and screw together the hinge and plate. Finally, fill the old holes on the door and unit and, if necessary, paint over them for a finish almost as good as new.

quick fix

As an alternative to cutting a new hinge, it may sometimes be possible to refix a hinge plate with the aid of some resin.

1 Remove the loosened hinge plate and then carefully expel some resin into the old fixing holes.

2 Reposition the hinge plate and screw it back in place, holding it in position until the resin 'goes off'. Excess resin will probably squeeze out around the edge of the hinge plate when it is screwed in place. Remove this with a cloth before it has the chance to dry. Rehang the door once the resin has fully hardened.

drawer problems

Whereas hinge problems are common for unit doors, the main problems encountered with drawers tend to relate either to the loosening of screw fixings for the handles or the drawer fronts themselves. In either case, adhesive can be used to reinforce fixings and return the drawers to good working order.

tools for the job

cordless drill/driver

clamps (optional)

screwdriver

fixing fronts

1 Drawer fronts often become loose, as the effectiveness of the screw fixings lessens with constant use. To remedy this problem, simply unscrew the drawer front and apply a generous amount of wood glue or pva to the back face.

2 Screw the front back onto the drawer carcass. It is important for the back face of the drawer front and the front face of the carcass to be pressed together very tightly, in order to ensure proper adhesion.

You may therefore need to attach some clamps to hold the front firmly in position. Although the screw fixings for the drawer front will remain slightly loose, the combined effect of the glue and screws will hold the drawer front back in the desired position.

fixing handles

1 Again, the daily opening and closing of drawers will take its toll on the screw fixings for handles, which may become loose or fall off completely. For obvious aesthetic reasons it will not be possible to reposition the handle and make new fixings altogether. To repair a loosened handle, therefore, you will need to unscrew it and apply a small amount of resin to the thread of the fixing bolt.

2 Screw the handle back in position using washers to help spread the force put on the handle when the drawer is opened. This technique can also be applied to door handles and handles with only one fixing point.

making tile repairs

Tile repairs can be applied to the two separate areas that make up the one tile surface – in other words the tiles themselves and the grout joints. Deterioration of either surface will let down the overall look of the kitchen and it is therefore important to address such problems in order to maintain kitchen appearance.

replacing a broken tile

tools for the job

cordless drill/driver

grout raker

protective equipment

hammer

cold chisel

scraper

dusting brush

adhesive spreader

A chipped or broken tile can let down the appearance of a complete tiled surface. In many cases the damage has been caused by a physical knock or blow of some nature, but much of the time slight weaknesses in tile structure at the time of manufacture can result in hairline cracks occurring at a later date. In either case, the technique for rectifying the situation is similar, and involves the complete removal of the damaged tile and replacement with a new one.

1 Some broken tiles may be so loose that they can literally be lifted away with the aid of a chisel or scraper. However in most cases you will find that the adhesive still holds all sections of the tile firmly in place. It therefore becomes necessary to weaken the tile structure further by drilling a number of holes in its surface. For this purpose attach a tile bit or a masonry bit to a cordless drill, but take care not to allow the bit to slip and damage surrounding tiles. Drill right through the tile until

the bit touches (or you judge it as touching) the wall surface below. This will help to break up the tile.

safety advice

The force used to knock old tiles out of position can cause splinters to fly in all directions. Therefore remember to wear the appropriate protective equipment – goggles are essential to protect the eyes.

2 To loosen further the tile, use a grout raker to remove the hard grout from around the edges. Dig out as much grout as possible, but again take care not to damage the edges of the surrounding tiles.

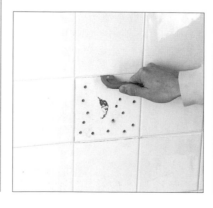

3 Use a hammer and cold chisel to knock out gradually the broken sections of tile. Once one section has been removed, it will be easier to position the point of the chisel directly onto the tile/wall junction, thus making it easier to lever out sections until the whole space has been cleared.

4 Try to remove any hardened adhesive remaining on the wall surface with the aid of a scraper. If this is ineffective, try to use the cold chisel to tap away the adhesive and take the surface back to wall. Leaving any protruding adhesive can cause a new tile to sit too proud and stand out from the tiled surface. Clean out any loose debris using a dusting brush.

5 With the broken tile and old adhesive completely removed, apply fresh adhesive to the new tile and press it into place. Insert spacers perpendicular to the tile surface, in order to maintain a consistent gap in which to apply the grout. It is a sensible idea at this stage to hold a small length of batten across the front of the new tile surface, overlapping onto the existing tiles, to check that it is positioned totally flush.

6 Once the adhesive has dried completely, you can remove the spacers and grout the joints in the usual way.

👍
tips of the trade

The most difficult part about tile replacement can often be finding a good colour match to blend with the other tiles. For this reason, on any new tiling project, it is always worth holding onto a few extra tiles so that, should any breakages occur in the future, a supply of tiles of the exact colour is available for use.

regrouting tiles

tools for the job

grout raker

dusting brush

vacuum

grout spreader

sponge

grout shaper (optional)

cloth

Dirty or worn grout can easily be replaced by simply scraping it out and replacing it with a new mix. As well as boosting the tile surface appearance, this task can be seen as renewing the waterproof properties of the surface.

1 Scrape out all the old grout using a grout raker. Dig the blade of the raker into the joints, but try not to damage the edge of any tiles during this process.

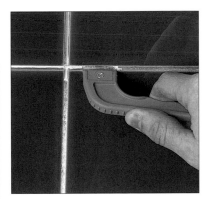

2 Clean out all the joints using a dusting brush and then vacuum along all the joints to ensure that no small particles of dust or grit are left between any of the tiles. Be as thorough as possible while you are doing this, as any stray grit and dust sitting between the tiles will contaminate the new grout application, affecting its smooth finish and creating weak spots for water penetration.

3 Apply the grout in the usual way (see page 105), pressing it in place firmly along all the joints. Remove any excess grout with a damp sponge as you work. In some cases, you may wish to 'tool' the joints with a grout shaper to provide an even neater finished look. Finally, polish the surface with a dry cloth.

OTHER TILE REPAIRS

The options for repair shown here may also be applied to worktop and floor tiles. With worktop tiles you will need to apply a pva solution to the exposed surface of the worktop before reapplying adhesive.

The main difference with floor tiles is that they are thicker and stronger than wall tiles, so you may need more heavyweight equipment, such as a power drill, to drill through the tile surface. Likewise, the grout in-between floor tiles will be harder than the equivalent in wall tiles. Thus this sort of job does tend to require a greater degree of physical exertion.

replacing taps & washers ⁄⁄⁄

During the working life of a tap the washers will almost certainly need to be replaced. In some cases total tap replacement may be required, either because the existing tap is too old and has seized up completely, or because a new look is desired.

Older or traditional-style tap designs tend to employ a system of rubber washers to form the seal between the head gear and the tap spout. Whereas modern taps may employ totally different proprietary systems. Cartridges are becoming more popular in tap design, and if problems occur the entire cartridge will need to be replaced. Tap design is therefore an important consideration when it comes to fixing leaks and drips.

replacing taps

Replacing a tap is a straightforward process, but remember to choose a design that is compatible with the existing sink – for example, if there is only one hole in the sink then choice will be restricted to a monobloc design – and try to ensure that the pipework required for reconnecting a new tap is also compatible with existing fixings.

tools for the job

adjustable spanners (optional)

slip-joint pliers

1 Turn off the water at the service valves. If the sink does not have separate service valves, then turn off supplies at the appropriate stopcocks. Turn on the taps to remove any water left in the pipes. Unscrew the backnut under the sink, which holds the tap and backwashers in place – it may

require loosening first with a spanner. Disconnect the supply pipes from the service valves. In modern systems, they are usually either threaded or secured with a compression joint, but with older systems you may need to cut through the pipes.

2 Lift out the old taps from the sink unit, pulling the supply pipes through the sink hole.

3 Attach the new supply pipes (in this example threaded tap connectors have been used) and position the sealing washer at the base of the new tap.

4 Secure the new tap in place with the backnut and washers supplied, and then connect it up to the existing supply. The connection may simply be threaded, or you might need to add a compression joint to create a watertight seal. Always refer to the manufacturer's guidelines for the specific design of tap connector being used. Turn the water supply back on once the tap is fully connected.

tips of the trade

Rather than having a sealing washer at the base of the tap, some designs may require a gasket to act as the seal or it may even be necessary to seat the taps on a bed of silicone sealant. All techniques are designed to create a seal so that water cannot leak through to the underside of the sink.

replacing washers

The following examples show the basic technique for renewing rubber washers, though the type of washer and way in which it is accessed and changed can vary according to tap design. Before replacing any type of washer, ensure the water supply has been turned off at a supply valve and/or at the mains.

tools for the job

screwdriver bit
screwdriver(s)
slip-joint pliers
adjustable spanners

spout washers

1 Undo the retaining grub screw that holds the spout in place. This is normally located at the rear of the tap, making access difficult. A screwdriver bit is a good tool for gaining access and undoing the screw.

2 Once the grub screw has been removed the spout can simply be lifted out. There are normally two washers at the base of the spout, one called the top sealing washer and the other generally referred to as the O-ring. Use the end of a screwdriver to prise off both these washers, and then simply stretch new washers into place.

headgear washers

These are the most common washers in need of replacement, and are situated deep inside the tap body on the end of the tap headgear.

1 Flip off the cap on the tap handle to reveal the retaining screw. Undo this screw to remove the handle.

2 Undo the tap shroud using a pair of slip-joint pliers. Protect the shroud from scratching by either covering the jaws of the pliers with a cloth or, as shown here, some masking tape.

3 With the headgear revealed, use an adjustable spanner to grip tightly onto the headgear and then unscrew it from its position. If the fitting is particularly tight, you may also need another spanner in order to hold the tap firmly in place.

4 Flip off the old washer at the base of the headgear with a screwdriver and push a new washer into place. In some cases you may find the washer has been secured with a small bolt or screw, which will need undoing to remove and fit the new washer. The tap may now be fixed back together, following the same procedure in reverse, and the water supply turned back on.

tips of the trade

It can sometimes be difficult to snap the new washer in place on the headgear. If this is the case, soften the washer in some warm water first to ease the process.

plumbing maintenance

By maintaining kitchen plumbing systems in good order, many more major problems can be avoided. Keeping drains clear and free from obstruction can prevent more damaging blockages, and observing whether water flows away quickly or slowly from the sink will provide an idea as to whether problems are ahead. It is therefore best to try to pre-empt major blockages, rather than react once they become serious.

using chemical cleaners

There are various chemical cleaners available on the market, most of which are caustic (generally containing sodium hydroxide), so protective gloves should always be used when handling them. Ideally, they are used when the first signs of a blockage begin to become apparent. In this way, they can dispel the material causing the blockage before it has a chance to build up to more damaging levels.

1 Read the manufacturer's guidelines carefully, but in general one or two spoonfuls of the cleaner need to be poured down the plug hole of the sink.

2 Run a small amount of water to ensure that none of the granules are allowed to rest on any exposed part of the sink bowl. Leave the cleaner to work for 20 minutes to half an hour before flushing the system out with more water. One further application may be required to clear the blockage, but if it still remains after

a second application it is likely that alternative methods may be required. Make sure there is adequate ventilation when carrying out this procedure as the fumes can be quite overpowering.

safety advice

For homes that have a septic tank as part of their drainage system, this type of chemical based caustic cleaner cannot be used. A bacteria-based treatment must be used instead.

using plungers

When chemical cleaners are ineffective, the next option to try is a simple sink plunger. The suction created between the plunger and the sink outlet puts pressure on the blockage and forces it out of position.

1 For the plunger to be effective, it is first necessary to create an airlock in the drainage system. This can be achieved by inserting a rag or cloth in the overflow outlet.

2 The plunger is then positioned over the sink outlet allowing the suction pad to create a secure seal around the outside of the plughole. If you are using a traditional plunger, simply push and pull up and down on the wooden handle to create the suction required to dislodge the blockage. In this example, however, a particularly modern design of plunger has been used, which works on a similar principle to traditional designs except in this case water is sucked into the plunger cylinder and forced at high pressure into the blockage below. Rhythmical moving up and down of the plunger handle should put enough pressure on the blockage to loosen it.

removing traps

If the options for dispelling a blockage at sink level are not successful, it may be necessary to turn your attention to below sink level and consider the drainage pipes and sink trap. It may, therefore, be necessary to undo the trap and clean it out by hand in order to remove a blockage.

1 Most traps simply unscrew by hand. For particularly stiff or solid joints, however, it may be necessary to use some slip-joint pliers to provide a good grip and extra leverage for undoing purposes. Before you start unscrewing, always position a bowl below the trap to catch any excess water inside.

2 Flush out the trap with water and use your fingers to remove any large pieces of material that could be contributing to the blockage. This can be a bit of a messy business, so you may wish to wear some gloves to protect your hands.

3 Before you replace the trap, you could take the opportunity to replace any washers in order to renew the seals.

using an auger

Augers are extremely effective tools for dealing with all manner of blockages, and where a sink is blocked, or rather a sink drainage system is blocked, an auger might be the best piece of equipment for rectifying the situation. The long spring and handle mechanism give you good access to the blockage and provide the force you will need to break it up and release it.

1 Remove the trap on the sink to leave access to the drainage pipe. Pull out the sprung section of the auger to a length that can be inserted into the drainage pipe. When removing the trap from the sink, remember to have a bowl close at hand to catch the excess water that will be released.

2 Insert the sprung section into the pipe and turn the handle of the auger so that it screws into the pipe void and eventually comes into contact with the blockage. Keep turning the auger handle to allow the sprung section to burrow into the blockage, gradually breaking it down, making it much easier to wash away down the pipe.

tips of the trade

Where a trap is 'weeping', or leaking water around the threaded section, if you are unable to find a suitably-sized replacement washer, it is possible to employ silicone sealant in order to stop the leak. Simply remove the section, dry it thoroughly, and apply sealant around the thread before screwing it back into position. Allow the sealant to dry before using the sink again.

MACHINE MAINTENANCE

Washing machines and dishwashers require little general maintenance, other than occasionally checking to ensure that the supply and drainage pipes are in good working order and that there are no visible leaks or drips. However, it is worth referring to the manufacturer's guidelines for the particular appliance as, for example, in some situations filters may need cleaning or replacing to enable the machine to function at optimum levels.

renovating an existing kitchen

It is not always the case that a complete kitchen refit is required to give a new lease of life to the room itself. In many cases, simple redecoration, the addition of further accessories or replacing the floor covering can help to revamp the look of a tired kitchen design. The superficial, rather than structural, elements are therefore a good focus for a general kitchen makeover. This chapter provides examples of different areas and surfaces in the kitchen, and how some slight renovations in these areas can help to transform the room's general appearance. As well as being far quicker than total renovation, making small changes that have maximum impact can also be the most economical way of providing a great new look to your kitchen.

A new colour scheme, change of worktop for the end cupboard and new tile splashback have given this kitchen a real face-lift.

changing worktop //////

When kitchen units are still in relatively good condition, but the worktop has suffered from years of wear and tear, it can be effective simply to change the worktop in order to revamp the kitchen's appearance. This is a very simple process on straight uninterrupted lengths, but where sinks or hobs have been cut into the worktop, the procedure becomes slightly more complicated.

tips of the trade

Before changing a worktop, check that the dimensions of the new length will fit the position of the existing length. This may appear obvious in terms of the depth and length of the worktop, but height must also be considered. For example, if the new worktop is of a greater height than the old one, it will not fit under the bottom row of tiles. If it is a lesser height, then it will fit but some sort of cover strip may be required to cover the larger gap at the back edge of the worktop. Also pipe lengths and/or connections may need to be reduced so that supplies can be turned back on. Therefore, be sure to double-check all such measurements before starting work.

tools for the job

tape measure

pencil

adjustable spanners

slip-joint pliers

craft knife

grout raker

jigsaw

cordless drill/driver

screwdriver

sealant dispenser or gun

1 First of all shut off the water supply and disconnect taps following the procedure described on pages 120–1. Also disconnect the sink waste. Before undoing any further fixings along the worktop, it is necessary to release the back edge of the worktop from the wall. Although there tend to be no physical fixings in this area, silicone sealant and/or grout can create a good bond between worktop and wall along this edge. Firstly, cut through the silicone sealant with a craft knife.

2 Use a grout raker to further break the seal along the back edge of the worktop. Work the tool all around the edge thoroughly. The more of this material that you are able to remove at this stage, the easier you will find it to shift the old worktop out of place.

3 You can now turn your attention to the screw fixings that are positioned on the underside of the worktop. Release all of the screws both at the back and front sections of the worktop.

4 Undo the screws holding in the retaining clips for the sink. You may wish to remove the doors for this.

5 The worktop and sink may now be eased away from the top of the units. Employ a helper to lift the worktop out of place entirely.

6 Remove the sink completely, and position the old worktop on top of the new length. In this way, the old worktop can be used as a template for fitting the new one. Draw guidelines along the back edge of the worktop and for refitting the sink. If you are replacing the sink as well as the worktop, then it is best to fit the full length of worktop first and then cut the new sink in position as shown on pages 72–3.

7 Use a jigsaw to cut along the guidelines in order to remove the section of worktop required for fitting the sink. To gain access points for the blade of the jigsaw, insert a flathead drill bit into a cordless drill and make holes in the worktop just inside the sink guideline. (Once you have successfully inserted the blade bring the saw out to the guideline.) As you are cutting, make sure that the worktop is well supported, so that the weight of the section being removed cannot fracture the edges of the cut and thereby damage the finished look.

8 Reposition the worktop. Again, you will probably need a helper to lift it and carefully lower it into place. Ensure that the worktop is correctly aligned, especially at the sink position, before using screw fixings on the underside to secure it back in place.

9 Insert the sink unit and reuse clips to hold it in place. You can now refit the taps, reconnect the waste and turn on the water supply. To finish off the job and guarantee a watertight seal, it will also be necessary to use a fresh bead of silicone sealant along the back edge of the worktop.

Replacing a worktop can totally change kitchen appearance providing an immaculate new working surface, while helping to lift the look of existing items and fittings.

changing doors & handles

The style of a kitchen is often created by the types of doors, drawer fronts and handles that have been used in its design. The carcasses themselves have little to do with the look of a kitchen, so in order to change style, as long as the carcasses are in a good state of repair, it only becomes necessary to make changes to the more obvious areas, such as cupboard fronts and/or handles. Changing handles is clearly a very economic way of altering kitchen look, whereas door and drawer front replacement is certainly more dramatic, but will greatly increase the cost.

design options

There are always many options to choose from when making such unit changes, and personal preference will be the determining factor in the choice you make. Below are just a few examples of cupboard fronts and handles, showing slightly different designs and finishes. Remember when making choices, especially with doors, ensure that the new ones will fit the existing units in your kitchen. Subtle differences in size may not be immediately obvious when choosing between manufacturers and you should always double-check that dimensions will be suitable.

DOORS

wooden panel door

laminated wood effect panel door

painted finish panel door

solid wood flush door

KNOBS

brass

wood

ceramic

porcelain

HANDLES

brass

wood

antique brass
drawer pull

brass drawer pull

brushed steel

tools for the job

cordless drill/driver
screwdriver
combination square
pencil
wood block

changing doors

Replacing doors is a simple process where the old ones may be unscrewed at the hinge and the new ones fitted. In some cases, it may be suitable to reuse the old hinges, but if there is a difference in manufacturer's designs, you may need to fit new ones. Likewise, the hinge plates themselves may need changing on the carcass unit.

changing handles

Nearly all kitchen handles are interchangeable in that manufacturer's differences tend not to create too many problems. If you are changing a knob to a handle, however, you will need to drill an extra hole and if you are changing a handle to a knob, you will need to fill the leftover hole and repaint the unit to conceal it.

simple changeovers

1 Firmly hold onto the knob, or handle, while you undo the retaining screw(s).

2 Position the new knob, or handle, and screw it in place. Start this process by hand before using a screwdriver for final tightening.

changing from knob to handle

1 Use a combination square to measure down from the existing hole to a position that mirrors the distance between the threaded fixing points on your chosen new handle.

2 Mark this position accurately – if it is out of place, the thread of the screw may not engage correctly with the thread of the handle.

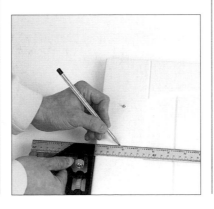

3 Drill through the marked off point. Be sure to position a block of wood on the other side of the door so that when the drill bit emerges it cannot split or 'blow out' the hole and damage the door side.

4 Line up the new handle over the drilled holes and tighten the fixings securely with a screwdriver.

DRAWER FRONTS

When you are replacing a drawer knob or handle, you may encounter a separate set of problems. Replacing one knob with another is a simple changeover, but it is more difficult to change a knob to a handle, as two new holes will require drilling, thus leaving a central hole in the drawer front. This creates another scenario whereby the drawer front must be painted in order to cover the old fixing holes. Even with a simple changeover of one handle for another you must check that the distance between the fixing holes is the same.

unit makeovers

As an alternative to replacing doors, handles or drawer fronts, it is possible to work on or add other finishes to existing units and fronts in order to change their appearance. As for all unit makeovers, it is important that the existing units are in a sound condition so that your efforts will be long lasting, and that adequate preparation is put into these tasks so that the finish itself is durable. Ideas and materials for unit makeovers are constantly being updated by manufacturers and below are just some examples of the options available.

adding panels

tools for the job

pencil

tape measure

combination square

cordless drill/driver

To increase interest on a flat or flush cupboard front, panels may be used to produce a more textured or three-dimensional finish. Mouldings may be bought and cut to length or, as shown here, proprietary kits may be purchased where the panels are already made up and simply require fitting. Although this latter technique adds a little expense, it does save a lot of time and ensures that the mitred corners of the panels are precise.

1 Use a pencil and combination square to measure the ideal position for fixing the panels to the doors. It is easier to remove doors and lay them out flat for this purpose.

2 Most panels are fixed in position with double-sided tape. Peel the tape off the back of the mouldings.

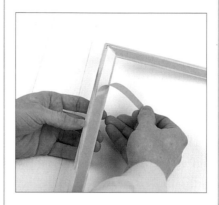

3 Position the mouldings so they are aligned with the pencil guidelines. The adhesive is very strong, but you can make any necessary minor adjustments in positioning before it finally sticks.

4 It is likely that the new moulding position may make it necessary to move handles. Simply remove the existing ones and fill in the screw holes. Then measure for an appropriate position to drill through the door and fix a new handle.

tips of the trade

• In order to get the best possible adhesion between the moulding and door, make sure that the door surface has been both thoroughly cleaned and well dried before you apply the panel.

• If you are using mouldings that are not fixed with self-adhesive tape, panel pins can be used to secure the mouldings in place. It can also be worth using a little pva adhesive on the back of the mouldings to add further strength to the fixing. The heads of the panel pins will need to be punched in and filled before you go on to decorate.

• Normally, the newly panelled door will require painting. Be sure to use esp to prepare the door surface if it is of a laminated or melamine finish. A varnished wooden door should be sanded back and primed before painting. If your preference dictates that panel colour is to be different to the background door colour, it is worth painting the panels and the doors separately before positioning the panels. In this way the dividing line between each will be as sharp as possible, and no time-consuming and fiddly cutting in will be required.

MOULDED UNITS

Instead of adding panels to flush doors, another method for producing a panelled effect is to use a router. By fitting the correct type of cutter, the router can be used to channel out a moulded pattern in the front of doors. This technique is for the more advanced woodworker.

covering doors

An alternative to adding mouldings to a flush door is simply to cover the whole face with a decorative wallpaper. There are companies that specifically manufacture for this purpose. Such paper is self adhesive and the technique for fitting is similar to that of general wallpapering.

tools for the job

tape measure & pencil
scissors
craft knife
sanding block
cordless drill/driver

1 Remove the handles and sand down the door surfaces to provide a key for the adhesive.

2 Use a damp sponge to wipe away any dust from the door surface and allow the surface to dry.

3 Use scissors to cut the paper to a size slightly longer than that of the door. (The width of the paper roll should be slightly greater than the door.) Peel back a small amount of the self adhesive backing paper and position the roll at the top of the door.

4 Gradually unroll the paper, pulling the backing away, and allowing the paper to stick to the door. Use the factory cut edge of one side of the length to follow the door edge.

5 Smooth the surface of the paper to remove any air bubbles, and use a craft knife to trim off any excess.

6 Use fine grade sandpaper to sand the edges of the door gently to ensure that the paper edges will not lift away from the surface.

7 Screw the handles in place. If you are changing handle design, fill the original holes before applying the paper, then drill new holes.

DRAWER UNITS

In both these examples, a door has been used for illustrative purposes. The same techniques may also be applied to drawer fronts in order to blend in the whole finish.

painting units

The degree of success in painting units is directly proportionate to the extent to which surfaces are prepared. Most kitchen units are varnished or of a laminate or melamine finish – none of which are good surfaces for direct paint application. However, modern primers and materials do now make it possible to apply paint successfully to these surfaces as long as the correct order of work is followed. Paint may be applied to provide a single colour or overall opaque finish. As an alternative a more distressed paint effect can be used to add further character to kitchen design.

preparing for paint

tools for the job

sponge

sandpaper

paintbrush

cloth

Proprietary primers or esp are the key materials for painting units. Before one of these can be applied, there are other steps in the preparation process that must be carried out. It can be easier to remove doors from units, as laying them down and painting the fronts flat will reduce the possibility of drips or runs in the finish.

1 The first, crucial stage is to give the area to be painted a thorough cleaning. Use a mild detergent solution to wash down the surfaces of the unit and remove any traces of dirt or grease from the door's surface. Rinse the door with clean warm water and allow it to dry.

2 Sand the entire door surface to provide a key for paint. Be sure to cover all areas and, where necessary, mould the piece of sandpaper to gain access to the more intricate shapes in panel doors.

3 Brush off the surface with a dusting brush and wipe it down once more to remove all traces of dust. Allow it to dry before applying a coat of esp using a paintbrush.

4 Wipe off the excess esp with a cloth and leave the remainder to dry. Once the surface of the door · is completely dry, you can begin to apply the paint finish.

distressing units

Paint effects are a good way of deviating from more traditional looks to provide texture to what would otherwise be a rather flat finish. Distressing creates a wonderful lived-in look for a homely feel – ideal for the kitchen environment. The preparation procedure for creating this effect is the same as demonstrated opposite, but when it comes to actual paint application, specific procedure must be followed to create the desired effect. A good distressed effect requires two main colours – so experiment to find the colour combination that suits you.

PRIME TIME

Esp and proprietary primers do vary in terms of application guidelines depending on the particular manufacturer. Take care to observe these instructions carefully as timing between application, removal and painting can be crucial to achieving a good overall finish.

tools for the job

paintbrush

sanding block

1 Apply a basecoat to the door, brushing out the paint thoroughly. Allow to dry and add a further coat.

2 Add dabs of petroleum jelly across the surface, paying close attention to edges and corner joints.

3 Paint a top coat on the door. Allow it to dry and reapply.

4 Once the second top coat has dried, use fine grade sandpaper across the entire surface of the door. Where the petroleum jelly has been applied, the paint will not have adhered properly and will therefore wipe away with the sandpaper. It can also be effective to be quite vigorous with your rubbing in places to provide a good contrast in finish.

5 Dust off the door and seal the finish with one or two coats of varnish. Once the varnish is dry, the door may be rehung.

MORE PAINT OPTIONS

• **Emulsion –** Use emulsion for painting the doors as it is quick drying and therefore allows a number of coats to be applied in the same day. An acrylic or water-based varnish may also be used for sealing purposes.

• **Petroleum jelly alternative –** Masking fluid can be used to achieve the same effects as petroleum jelly.

• **Exposing wood –** To create an even more distressed look, apply petroleum jelly before the base coat so that the bare door surface shows through.

133

Painted units provide warmth and comfort in a kitchen adding both colour and harmony to an overall kitchen scheme.

changing splashbacks ⟋⟋

A kitchen splashback refers to the entire wall area above the junction between a worktop and wall surface, not merely those areas above hobs or sinks. Splashbacks endure a large amount of abrasion, and for this reason they often need revamping or replacing well before the rest of the kitchen. Changing a splashback for another type of finish is also a relatively inexpensive means of changing the look of your kitchen without major renovation.

glass

The minimalist look of a glass splashback is becoming increasingly common. Manufacturers tend to supply them with a proprietary fixing kit making installation very simple.

tools for the job

tape measure
pencil
cordless drill/driver
Allen key
screwdriver

1 Mark off the precise dimensions of the glass splashback on the wall behind the hob. This is to ensure the splashback will be central to the position of the cooktop.

2 Hold the splashback in place against the wall and mark the fixing positions through the pre-drilled holes in the glass. Exactness is vital in this situation, for if any of the fixing points are inaccurately marked, this will risk damaging the glass when it comes to securing it in place.

3 Remove the splashback and drill holes in the wall at the marked off positions using a suitable drill bit.

4 This type of splashback is fixed with metallic plugs. Screw the plugs into the wall with an Allen key.

5 Before attaching the splashback to the wall with mirror screws, first position rubber washers over the screws to protect the glass as they are driven in place. Do not overtighten the screws. For this reason it is best to use a hand held screwdriver, which offers greater control.

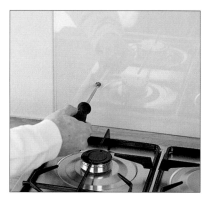

6 Fit the caps supplied onto the mirror screw heads to complete the splashback.

tips of the trade

Remember to paint the wall surface before attaching the splashback, as the wall finish will still show through the glass once positioned.

stainless steel

A stainless steel splashback offers a direct alternative to glass. Although steel is not as fragile as glass, take care fitting the splashback as it can be dented or scratched relatively easily. Retain any protective coating until it is fixed in position.

tools for the job

tape measure
pencil
cordless drill/driver
screwdriver

1 Measure and position two fixing brackets on the wall surface above the hob. The position of the brackets should correspond to the level indicated on the back of the stainless steel splashback.

2 Hook the back of the splashback over the brackets, simultaneously sliding its bottom edge down behind

the junction between work surface and wall. You may find the wall brackets need to be tightened or loosened off to allow the splashback to fit flush against the wall.

3 Once in position, remove the protective layer to reveal the stainless steel splashback effect.

tiles

tools for the job

tape measure
pencil
tile cutter
notched spreader
grout spreader
paintbrush

tiling over tiles

Apply tiles with the normal technique, maintaining gaps with spacers. Offset the new grout joints to reduce the risk of the grout lines cracking.

painting tiles

1 First sand the tile surface to provide a key, and then wash it down to remove any impurities.

2 Apply tile primer across the splashback surface. Leave to dry before applying any tile paint.

SPLASHBACK ALTERNATIVES

● **Work surface** – Use leftover worktop material as a splashback. It will be durable, easy-to-clean and consistent with the kitchen decoration.

● **Tile transfers** – A plain tile splashback can be revamped by using decorative tile transfers.

● **Mirrors** – Instead of using a glass splashback, consider using mirrors. This is especially effective in small kitchens where it can help to give an impression of space.

● **Mosaics** – A mosaic splashback creates a beautiful kitchen focal point.

glossary

Base unit – a kitchen unit that is sited at floor level.

Boxing in – technique of employing a framework to cover up unsightly items, such as pipes. Usually constructed out of a frame from wooden battens and covered with building board, such as mdf.

Breakfast bar – length of worktop which is used both for food preparation and for serving meals. Incorporates a seating facility created by an overhang on one or more sides.

Carcass – the basic structure of a kitchen unit where no embellishments such as doors or drawer fronts have been added.

Carousel – circular shelving system used in corner units that rotates in order to aid access.

Caulk – flexible filler supplied in tubes and dispensed from a sealant gun. Must be smoothed before it dries.

Cavity wall – wall composed of two layers. In effect, two walls separated by cavity or void. Common in construction of external walls of modern homes.

Ceiling unit – kitchen unit that is fixed to the ceiling.

Chipboard – flooring material made of compressed wooden fibres. Supplied in sheets, which are normally joined with a tongue and groove mechanism.

Colourizer – concentrated colour supplied in small tubes or containers, designed to add colour to paint or scumble for paint effect purposes. Some are universal in that they can be added to both acrylic and solvent based paints or glazes.

Concrete anchor – screw designed to fix into masonry without the need for a wall plug.

Cornice – decorative moulding fixed around the top edge of wall units.

Cutting in – term that refers to the method of painting in the corners or at the different junctions on a wall surface or between walls and ceilings.

Distressing – paint effect designed to give surfaces an aged look.

Dummy drawer front – drawer front that is not attached to a drawer but is fixed to a unit carcass to imitate drawer position in order to maintain the decorative finish of a run of units.

Eggshell – hardwearing paint that has a dull matt finish. Available in acrylic or solvent based forms.

Emulsion – acrylic or water-based paint used for open areas such as walls and ceilings.

End panel – decorative panel attached to the exposed sides of both wall and base units at the end of a run of units. Panel often matches finish of door fronts.

Esp – or 'easy surface preparation', a primer applied to laminate, melamine and tiled surfaces.

External corners – the corners that stick out into a room.

Extractor fan and hood – kitchen ventilation system that is housed in a decorative unit designed to imitate the appearance of a chimney. Positioned directly over a hob at a set distance in order to remove steam and cooking fumes.

Factory cut edge – a cut edge that has been produced as a result of the manufacturing process and is therefore cut with precision. When arranging worktop as far as possible the exposed edges should be factory cut edges rather than those cut by hand.

Fitted – term used to describe a kitchen that comprises similar units fixed in a permanent position, usually integrated together in 'runs'.

Flat-pack – also known as 'self-assembly', a kitchen unit supplied in sections that needs to be assembled before fitting in place. Name refers to the mode of packaging for delivery.

Flux – cleaning material used on joints prior to soldering.

Galley kitchen – term referring to a long narrow kitchen with units on opposing walls, similar in design to a 'u-shaped' kitchen.

Glaze – medium that colourizers are added to in order to create paint effects. Acrylic or solvent based alternatives. Sometimes referred to as scumble.

Grout – waterproof compound which fills the gap between tile joints.

Hard tile – ceramic wall or floor tiles as opposed to softer varieties such as cork or vinyl.

Headgear – term denoting the internal mechanism of a tap.

Internal corners – the corners that point away from the centre of a room.

Island unit – single unit or run of units positioned in the centre of a room, which are separate from the units around the perimeter of the room.

Joist – length of wood used in the construction of ceilings and floors.

Joist detector – sensor device used for finding the position of joists in ceilings or walls. Some may also have a different mode that can be employed to trace the position of electric cables or pipes, hence it is an important safety tool to help avoid drilling or nailing into pipes and cables.

Junction box box in which electrical cables are joined together.

Laminate – term used to describe the process whereby a thin plastic layer is bonded to another surface, such as fibreboard to create a kitchen worktop.

Lath – wooden laths are lengths of wood used in the make up of old walls before the invention of plasterboard.

L-shaped – term used to describe the layout of a kitchen that resembles the shape of an 'L'. In other words, the units extend from one wall around to the adjacent one.

Mdf – or medium density fibreboard. Building board made from compressed wooden fibres.

Mitre – angled joint, normally involving two lengths of material joining at a right angle, hence each piece must be cut at a 45° angle.

Monobloc – tap comprising one spout rather than two, where hot and cold water is mixed to provide the required temperature.

Open plan – home design where rooms are either spacious, or where smaller rooms have been knocked through to form one large room. Term is most often applied to kitchen design when walls have been knocked through to combine dining area and kitchen.

Pelmet and cornice – decorative moulding fixed around the bottom edge and top edge of wall units to provide a neat finish.

Peninsula unit – kitchen unit that extends out from a run of units fitted against a wall into the centre of the room, but is still integrated into the run. Storage areas and worktop may thus be accessed from both sides.

Plinth – board attached between the underside of base units and the floor to create a decorative finish, often clipped onto the feet of units using special brackets.

Ply – thin veneers of wood bonded together to create building board. The grain of alternate veneers tends to run at right angles to one another.

Primer – type of paint used to seal surfaces before adding further coats.

Proprietary – referring to a material, tool or technique that relates specifically to one manufacturer or group of manufacturers.

Ptfe – polytetrafluoroethylene tape used for mending leaking joints.

Pva – all-purpose adhesive that may also be used diluted with water to form a stabilising solution for powdery wall, ceiling and floor surfaces.

Resin – extra-strong adhesive.

Sealant – any tubed silicone or mastic for sealing along joints such as those between walls and window frames.

Self-levelling compound – compound applied to concrete floors in order to provide a level surface for further floor covering.

Silicone – waterproof sealant used along junctions.

Single run – kitchen layout where units are aligned along one wall.

Skirting board – decorative wooden moulding applied at base of wall.

Soft tile – decorative tiles made from pliable materials such as cork or vinyl.

Solvent based – or oil-based. Term used when referring to the make up of paint or glaze.

Spacer – divider used between ceramic tiles to keep consistency of distance between each of the tiles.

Splashback – area on wall surface directly above the worktop in a kitchen, especially behind a hob, which has been covered over with an easily wipeable material, such as tiles, stainless steel or glass.

Stud – wooden uprights used in the construction of a stud wall.

Stud wall – wall consisting of wooden studs and covered in plasterboard. Used as partition wall in houses.

Subfloor – the base floor material beneath a floor covering, usually either wooden floorboards or chipboard, or concrete.

Tongue and groove – interlocking mechanism used to join some types of planking, building or panelling board.

Traps – area directly below drainage outlet where waste is typically directed through a u-shaped section of pipe.

Unfitted – term used to describe kitchen layout where units are not permanently fixed.

U-shaped – description of kitchen layout where the units are arranged to mimic a u-shape.

Vinyl – man-made substance used to produce decorative, easy-to-clean floor coverings. Protective covering on some wallpapers or additive used in paint, to improve their hardwearing and wipeable properties.

Wall plug – plastic or metal sheath, inserted into pre-drilled hole in wall to house screw.

Wall units – kitchen cabinets mounted on wall surfaces.

Washer – small rubber rings used to prevent water leaking from joints within taps.

Window dressing – decorative finish for windows e.g. curtains and blinds.

Wood glue – adhesive for joining together wooden sections.

index

useful contacts

suppliers

The authors and publisher would like to thank the following companies:

B&V Masonry
Shothanger Works
Kingsclear Road
Wootton St Lawrence
Basingstoke
Hampshire
RG23 8TH
Tel. 01256 850987
for stone worktops

Bliss (Flights of Fancy) Ltd
Paradise Works
Arden Forest Estate
Alcester
Warwickshire
B49 6EH
Tel. 01789 400077
www.blisscatalogue.co.uk
for props

CJ Worksurfaccs
CJ Industrial Woodworking Ltd
Unit 7
Novers Hill Trading Estate
Bedminster
Bristol, BS3 5QY
Tel. 0117 953 1176
for corian® worktops

Dulux Decorator Centres
Tel. 0161 9683000
for paint

H-A Interiors
(Division of Cova Products Ltd)
Station Road
Cramlington
Northumberland, NE23 8AQ
Tel. 01670 718222
for Fablon to cover kitchen units

Hewden Plant Hire
Tel. 0161 8488621

Hillarys Blinds Limited
Colwick Business Park
Private Rd. No. 2
Nottingham, NG4 2JR
Tel. 0800 716 564
www.hillarys.co.uk
for blinds

Longpré Furniture Ltd
The Claddings
Station Road
Bruton
Somerset, BA10 0EH
Tel. 01749 813966
www.longpre.co.uk
for wooden worktops

MFI
Southon House
333 The Hyde
Edgware Road
Colindale
London, NW9 6TD
Tel. 0208 2008000
www.mfi.co.uk
for kitchen units and fittings

Screwfix Direct
Tel. 0500 414141
www.screwfix.com
for tools and fixings

Travis Perkins Trading Co. Limited
Tel. 01604 752424
building materials

associations

National Home Improvement Council
Tel. 020 78288230

Builders Merchants Federation
Tel. 020 74391753
advice on building materials and lists of suppliers

Electrical Contractors Association
Tel. 020 73134800

Federation of Master Builders
Tel. 020 72427583

Health and Safety Executive
Tel. 0541 545500

Heating and Ventilating Contractors Association
Telephone number as for Electrical Contractors Association

Hire Association Europe
Tel. 0121 3777707
equipment hire

Institute of Plumbing
64 Station Lane
Hornchurch
Essex, RM12 6NB
Tel. 01708 472791

Institution of Electrical Engineers
Savoy Place
London, WC2R 0BL
Tel. 020 72401871

Institution of Structural Engineers
Tel. 020 72354535

Kitchen Specialists Association
PO Box 311
Worcester, WR1 1DN
Tel. 01905 726066

Royal Institute of British Architects
Tel: 020 75805533

the authors

Julian Cassell and Peter Parham have run their own building and decorating business for several years, having successfully renovated a variety of large and small scale properties around the UK. These award-winning authors have written a number of books covering all aspects of DIY, and their innovative approach has made them popular television and radio guests.

acknowledgements

We would like to thank the following individuals for supplying props, advice and general help throughout the production of this book – Craig Rushmere, John and Margaret Dearden, David House at Hewden Hire in Bruton, Michael and Sue Read, Bill Dove and all the staff at the MFI showroom in Yeovil.

At Murdoch Books we would like to extend our gratitutude to all those who have helped put this book together, but special thanks are due to Alastair Laing and Iain MacGregor for dealing with all our problems with their customary ease.

Also, a big thank you to Tim Ridley for not only his expertise behind the camera, but also his contributions in front of it. Grazie mille to Marina Sala, his more than able assistant, and, as always, many thanks to Adele for her expertise in both the catering and consultation departments.

The Publisher would like to give special thanks to MFI, Shanks Armitage and Screwfix.

First published in 2001 by Murdoch Books UK Ltd
Copyright© 2001 Murdoch Books UK Ltd

ISBN 1 85391 948 9
A catalogue record for this book is available from the British Library.

All photography by Tim Ridley and copyright Murdoch Books UK Ltd except: p5 right MFI (Smeg), p6 bottom left MFI (Hygena), p7 MFI (Schreiber), p8 MFI (Hygena), pp10–11 MFI (Hygena), pp20–21 MFI (Hygena), p22 left MFI (Schreiber) right MFI (Hygena), p23 top right MFI (Schreiber) bottom right MFI (Hygena), p31 fridge/freezer MFI (Smeg) microwave and recycling bin MFI, p32 top MFI bottom MFI (Hygena), p33 left and bottom right MFI (Hygena) top right MFI (Schreiber), pp38–9 MFI (Hygena), p65 MFI (Hygena), pp68–9 Murdoch Books®/Meredith, p70 left MFI (Armitage) right MFI (Schreiber), p71 left and top right MFI (Hygena) bottom right MFI (Schreiber), pp80–1 Murdoch Books®/Meredith, pp82–3 all MFI (Hygena), p87 bottom right MFI (Hygena), pp94–5 MFI (Hygena), p96 left MFI (Hygena), p97 top right MFI (Hygena) bottom right MFI (Schreiber), p111 bottom right MFI (Hygena), pp112–3 MFI (Schreiber), pp124–5 MFI (Hygena), p133 bottom right Murdoch Books®/Meredith

Commissioning Editor: **Iain MacGregor**
Series Editor: **Alastair Laing**
Designer: **Shahid Mahmood**
Managing Editor: **Anna Osborn**

Design Manager: **Helen Taylor**
Photo Librarian: **Bobbie Leah**
Photographer: **Tim Ridley**
Illustrations: **Mike Badrocke**

CEO: **Robert Oerton**
Publisher: **Catie Ziller**
Production Manager: **Lucy Byrne**
International Sales Director: **Kevin Lagden**

Colour separation by Colourscan, Singapore
Printed in Singapore by Tien Wah Press

Murdoch Books UK Ltd
Ferry House, 51–57 Lacy Road, Putney,
London, SW15 1PR, UK
Tel: +44 (0)20 8355 1480
Fax: +44 (0)20 8355 1499
Murdoch Books UK Ltd is a subsidiary of
Murdoch Magazines Pty Ltd.

UK Distribution
Macmillan Distribution Ltd
Houndsmills, Brunell Road
Basingstoke, Hampshire, RG1 6XS, UK
Tel: +44 (0) 1256 302 707
Fax: +44 (0) 1256 351 437
http://www.macmillan-mdl.co.uk

Murdoch Books®
GPO Box 1203
Sydney, NSW 1045, Australia
Tel: +61 (0)2 8220 2000
Fax: +61 (0)2 8220 2020
Murdoch Books® is a trademark of
Murdoch Magazines Pty Ltd.